GOLF
The History of an Obsession

AVBREY
BEARDSLEY

GOLF

The History of an Obsession

DAVID STIRK

Phaidon Press Limited, Littlegate House, St Ebbe's Street, Oxford OX1 1SQ

Distributed in the United States, under special arrangement, by
Price Stern Sloan, Inc. 360 N. La Cienega Blvd, Los Angeles, California 90048

First published 1987
© Phaidon Press Limited 1987

ISBN 0-89586-752-4

Picture research by Jenny de Gex

Printed in Spain by Heraclio Fournier SA, Vitoria

Captions to illustrations

(p.1) Fashion plate designed by Aubrey Beardsley for an invitation card for a
women's golf club in Mitcham, Surrey, 1894.

(p.2) *A Tour in Italy: Roman Campagna*, 1920s print by Edina Vittorio Accornero.

(p.3) Clark Stanton's preparatory oil study for the frontispiece to R. Clark *Golf, a
Royal and Ancient Game*, 1893.

(p.5) Arthur Rackham engraving, from R. H. Lyttelton *Outdoor Games, Cricket and
Golf*, 1906.

Contents

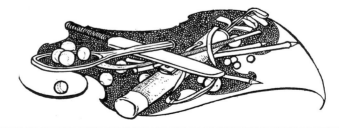

Paul Bril: *A Game of Jeu de Mail*, 1624. The painting shows this early game being played in open country near Rome. As in golf, there is a teeing ground, and the players are discussing the line of the shot. On the right two customers attend the 'pro's shop', where clubs are on display and a ballmaker is plying his trade.

The First Golfers

James Barclay, *The Swilcan Bridge, St Andrews*, etching, c.1920.

When and where did golf begin? No one knows, but given Man's propensity for throwing, rolling and kicking balls, and hitting them with various bats, rackets, clubs and cues, the development of the notion of hitting a small stationary ball across turf with a stick for fun was inevitable. Probably the game evolved independently in different places and at different times, developing along local lines and being played by groups of people who were unaware of each other.

Written records show that in Scotland a game called, variously, goff, gowf or golf was being played as early as 1457. A proclamation of that date by James II of Scotland forbade by Royal Decree the playing of 'futeball' and 'gowf' because they interfered with the much more important practice of archery. Skilled archers were vital to the defence of the Realm.

That a Royal Decree was necessary to damp down enthusiasm for the games shows not merely that golf and football were being played in fifteenth-century Scotland but that they had achieved nationwide popularity. Thus, though there are no earlier records of golf being played, it was clearly well established by the 1450s.

In 1501 the Treaty of Glasgow was signed, bringing peace between Scotland and England. Doubtless it had been Scotland's earlier fear of England that had made the training of Scottish archers so important, for shortly after the signing of the Treaty James IV of Scotland relaxed enough to start playing golf himself, and the Lord High Treasurer of Scotland recorded the purchase of clubs and balls from Perth for the King's use. The long association between the Stuart kings and the game of golf had begun.

References to golf and to matters concerning it appear with growing frequency in the records of succeeding years. One of the more dramatic of these relates to the trial of Mary, Queen of Scots, at which it was charged that she played at pall mall and golf only a few days after the murder of her husband, Lord Darnley.

In 1603, with the union of the two kingdoms, King James VI of Scotland became also James I of England, and proceeded to London accompanied by a large retinue of courtiers and their families. One result of this migration was the introduction of golf into England, in particular in the London area.

In 1604 a William Mayne was appointed Royal Clubmaker. In those days the Royal Court occupied Greenwich Palace, and a contemporary manuscript in

(left) Lemuel Abbott's engraving of 1778, dedicated to 'The Society of Goffers at Blackheath', shows William Innes, Blackheath's captain. The caddie, a Greenwich Hospital pensioner, carries a sustaining bottle of spirits as well as clubs.

An early Dutch form of golf, shown in a Flemish Book of Hours of the sixteenth century. The golf hole in the ground is an unusual feature – the game was more commonly played on ice at this period.

(below) The 'Crécy Window', a fourteenth-century stained-glass roundel in Gloucester Cathedral, one of the earliest representations of golf or of one of its precursors.

Adriaen Van de Velde: *Winter Landscape, Golfers on the Ice near Haarlem*, 1668. A Dutch landscape, but Scottish golfers, distinguishable by their kilts.

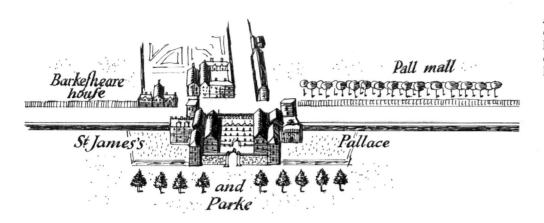

A seventeenth-century map by the cartographers Faithorne and Newcourt indicates the Pall Mall court near St James's Palace, London.

the Harleian Library describes James I's son Henry playing golf on the Black Heath, the area immediately adjacent to Greenwich, on the River Thames. While this written evidence concerns only Henry, certainly other members of the Court must also have played there. For more details of this the reader is referred to *Royal Blackheath*, by Henderson and Stirk.

Though golf came to England in the early seventeenth century a game very like it was being played by Englishmen long before that. The evidence for this is a roundel in the great east window of Gloucester Cathedral, sometimes called the 'Crécy window'. The roundel, dated about 1350, shows a man wielding a golf club of sorts and holding it in a typical golfer's grip, though the ball seems rather large for a golf ball.

There is a theory that golf-like games evolved independently in different parts of the world. Certainly it is clear from historical records that a number of stick-and-ball games were played in different parts of the British Isles from the earliest times, games such as hurley in Ireland and shinty in Scotland. But in these the ball was struck while it was in motion, and they were team games played at goals, not holes. There are also references to 'cambuca', a very early English game played with a stick and ball, but we know nothing of it or how it was played.

Because of the many games that are somewhat like golf one may ask 'What *is* golf?' The *Concise Oxford Dictionary* defines it as 'a game for two persons, or couples, in which a small hard ball is struck with clubs, having wooden or metal heads, into each of a series of holes on smooth greens at varying distances apart and separated by fairways, rough, hazards, etc., the object being to hole the ball in the fewest possible strokes.' Other dictionaries differ from this definition only in small details; all agree on the fundamental object of hitting a ball with sticks into a hole in the ground with as few strokes as possible.

In the light of this definition it is interesting to consider some other games that bear a distinct, if superficial, resemblance to golf.

Pall Mall, *jeu de mall* or *pele mele*

This stick-and-ball game, already mentioned in connection with Mary, Queen of Scots, was first played in Italy, but it was taken up by the French, who developed it, and it is generally thought of as a French game. It was played in

(below) Frontispiece and (below right) title page from *Nouvelles Regles pour le Jeu de Mail*, published by Huguier and Cailleau, Paris, 1717. Here a man with a short club seems to play with a small ball while carrying a larger one. We don't know why, nor whether he would have played one- or two-handed.

Comme on doit estre quand on ti à la passe pour finir la parti. p
a Paris Chez le Sr de Mortain Sur le pont Nostre L.

A collection of early clubs and balls. The long club was probably used for *colf*. The *jeu de mail* club on the left resembles a croquet mallet. The two spoon-shaped clubs on the right and the three wooden balls are for use in *chole*.

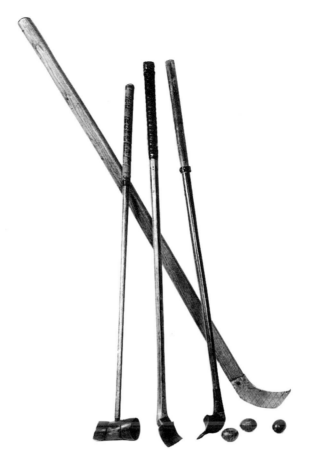

NOUVELLES
REGLES
POUR LE JEU
DE
MAIL.

TANT SUR LA MANIERE
d'y bien joüer, que pour décider
les divers évenemens qui peuvent
arriver à ce Jeu.

A PARIS,

Chez {
C H A R L E S H U G U I E R,
Imprimeur-Libraire, ruë Saint
Jacques, à la Sageſſe.
E T
A N D R E´ C A I L L E A U, Quay
des Auguſtins, près la ruë
Pavée, à Saint André.

MDCCXII.
AVEC PRIVILEGE DU ROY.

Scotland from the sixteenth century – perhaps a result of the then close Scottish-French affinity – and introduced into England in the seventeenth century.

Pall mall clubs resemble golf clubs, and the few pictures we have show that the player's swing was very like a golf swing. The game was played in a well-defined court, and at its end it was necessary to hit the ball through a hoop. The largest such court in Europe was the *pele mele* court at St James's, London, where, it is known, Charles I played in 1629; it was 1,000 yards long. When the game ceased being played there in the mid-eighteenth century the court became the road between what is now Trafalgar Square and St James's Palace, a road still known as Pall Mall. The game died out about the same time in the rest of Europe, except in France, where a cross-country version, *jeu de mail à la chicane*, was popular. In this the ball was struck across fields and along country lanes, ending at a definite target, such as a church or barn door.

Another game involving clubs and balls similar to golf balls and, so far as we know, a golf type of swing was *chole*, played in Flanders from mediaeval times, and its French version, *soule*, in which a beechwood ball was played across country to a certain target tree or door. There were several players on each side, making it something of a team game. One team was allowed three shots toward the target – the *chole* – and the opposing team was then allowed one shot in the opposite direction, the *dechole*.

Enough has been said to show that, whatever the similarities of clubs and swings, these games did not constitute golf within the dictionary definition. But when we come to a certain Dutch game similarities become more pronounced and greater care in definition is needed.

This seventeenth-century painting is one of the earliest illustrations of golf being played at St Andrews. At the right of the picture can be seen the Swilcan bridge, which is still a feature of the old golf course.

Hendrik Avercamp: *A Winter Scene with Skaters on Ice*. Golf has always had its hazards. In this bustling scene the *colf* players must have been severely restricted, not to mention the danger they themselves posed to innocent bystanders.

1. *Colf* was first played 600 years ago. This eighteenth-century woodcut shows early clubmakers at work.

Het Kolven

Golf seems to have started simultaneously, with certain local differences, in Holland and Scotland, and *het kolven* emerges out of a confused nomenclature as a generic term for the early Dutch game. But the modern historian of Dutch golf, Steven van Hengel, preferred two other names: *colf* for the game played before 1800 and *kolf* thereafter. The games were distinctly different.

The earlier *colf* was played over open country, sometimes along rural roads and often on frozen lakes and rivers. Indeed there are more pictures extant of it being played on ice than otherwise, which suggests that it was regarded very much as a winter game. There were no 'holes' in *colf*; instead the participants played towards agreed 'targets' such as trees or mill doors. On ice the target would be a peg frozen into place.

Sometimes the fortunes of a game would take its players through city streets, leaving a trail of injuries and broken windows that eventually led to *colf* being banished to the surrounding countryside.

Colf died out rather mysteriously during the eighteenth century, and the *kolf* that replaced the boisterous cross-country game was quite different, a sort of mini-*colf*, played much less strenuously in a courtyard, often a covered one with an inn handily nearby where the players could get a drink.

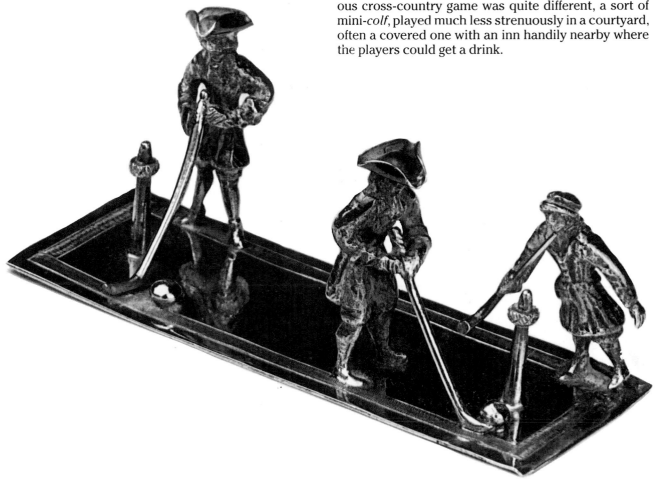

2. An eighteenth-century Dutch silver miniature showing men playing *kolf*, the more decorous game that replaced *colf*.

3. A fashionable *kolf* court in eighteenth-century Amsterdam.

4. *(far left)* Reproduction of an early plate showing *colf* in 1719. The tee is a heap of snow, the 'target' a door or tree.

5. This silver dish features an early colfer and his dog. The man's dress supports the notion that *colf* was a winter game.

17

Spel metten kolve

The late, lamented Steven van Hengel, of Holland, was the historian par excellence of this game. An indefatigable and painstaking researcher, he established the facts and discarded the mythology. His book *Early Golf* is the definitive work on the game in Holland and is recommended to anyone seeking a really authoritative description of the *spel metten kolve* and its history.

According to van Hengel the game was played in Holland from very early times. Much of its earlier history is derived from ordinances designed to protect the public from the players, and in these the game is referred to by several different names. *Spel metten kolve* is the commonest, but others that occur are *colf*, *colven* and *kolven*. In *Early Golf* van Hengel calls this ancient form *colf*.

There is a clear similarity here between the names. Certainly there is no word in the Scottish language resembling 'golf' until the name gowf or goff was used in the Royal Decree of 1457, whereas *colf* was played in Holland, according to records, from 1297. Van Hengel points out that there was much (well-documented) interaction between Holland and Scotland from 1485 to the seventeenth century and close ties between the countries right up to the eighteenth. Large numbers of feather balls were sent from Holland to Scotland and wooden clubs travelled in the opposite direction. One strength of the Dutch history of *colf* is the beautifully kept documentation. Another lies in the fact that the Dutch landscape painters of the fifteenth, sixteenth and seventeenth centuries frequently depicted *colf* being played, usually on ice. A painting of 1668 shows two kilted Scotsmen playing *colf* on ice in Holland. However, it does not seem that the Scots ever tried to play on ice in their own

Hendrik Avercamp's *Golf on Ice on the River Ijsel near Kampen*, in chalk, ink and watercolour, is a typical seventeenth-century Dutch winter 'golfing' scene.

In this *Winter Landscape* painted
by Aert van der Neer the colfers
are playing to a stake in the ice.

country. Theirs was a spring and autumn game, and to some extent a summer game played on short seaside turf.

To sum up, in Scotland and Holland the same feather ball was used and the clubs were somewhat similar, though the Dutch seem to have used lead or iron heads, of a different shape from those on Scottish clubs and fixed to the wooden shaft in a different manner. The Dutch paintings show few wooden-headed clubs, and those few were probably imports from Scotland. In short, the balls were the same, the clubs similar and the two names, golf and *colf*, very close.

Dissimilarities are equally clear. In *Early Golf* van Hengel defines golf as: '...a game in which a player stands alongside the line of play and strikes a ball with a club, a) for the lowest number of strokes from one point to another, or b) for the greatest distance for an agreed number of strokes.' This does not tally with the dictionary definition.

The differing Dutch and Scottish forms of the game were probably developments of earlier stick-and-ball games evolving independently, their differences being due to different terrains and climates. That the names were similar is very likely because the Scots took their version from the Dutch. Probably of earlier origins than the Scottish game, the Dutch one would have been familiar to the Scots, exchanging as they did the balls and clubs common to both.

The game of *colf* flourished in Holland, reaching its zenith in the seventeenth century. Holland was a great maritime nation at the time, with colonies round the world, and many *colf* players took their clubs and balls with them when they went abroad. There are pictures of colf players in Rome in 1622 and at Cleve, in Germany, in 1660. Within the past two years *colf* clubs have been found in the wreck of a Dutch 'East Indiaman' sunk off Stornaway in the early seventeenth century *en route* to Batavia, in the Dutch East Indies (now Indonesia).

Colf also crossed the Atlantic, and records – in the form of ordinances to protect the public – show that it was being played in the area of Fort Orange, now Albany, N.Y. in 1659. It appeared in America 100 years before Scots golf was recorded there.

In view of its great popularity it is surprising that in the early eighteenth century, suddenly and for no clear reason, the game of *colf* ceased to be played. In its place there arose a game that van Hengel calls *kolf*. This game is often mistakenly referred to as *het kolven* and is thought, just as erroneously, to be a form of golf. In fact it was a form of mini-*colf* and was played in a small, often covered, courtyard. But the form of the game altered too, making it more like *jeu de mail* – also very popular in Holland – than *colf*.

To return to the Scots game of golf: there is no doubt that golfing activity continued in the seventeenth century but there were few to write about it, and as landscape painting in Britain did not develop for a further 100 years we have no contemporary pictures of the game, unlike the Dutch and their *colf*. There are sporadic references: bills for golfing expenses in 1628, records of the names of ballmakers and clubmakers, and in 1640, it is recorded, Charles I played golf at Newcastle as a prisoner of the Scots. Later in the century we have the legendary match in which James, Duke of York – later to be King James II – played with John Patersone against two Englishmen. This match is discussed on page 96.

So golf was certainly being played, but it would seem to have been more of

The title page of *A New Game of Golf*, a Dutch play by D. Schuurman published in 1782, shows two *kolf* courts. The game contrasts sharply with the *colf* seen on pp.18-19.

Golfers in Rome, 1622. A lyrical depiction by Cornelis van Poelenburgh of the game played *à la chicane* amid ancient ruins.

The famous Castle broods distantly in *Edinburgh from Bruntsfield Links*. Strictly speaking the course, shown here as it was in 1798, is not a true links.

a Royal Court game than one for ordinary citizens. This was not because it was not popular, as some have suggested, but because it was expensive. A feather ball cost three times as much as a club and it was necessary to have three or four in one's pocket while playing. This was not only because a ball could get lost; it could also burst easily, or it could become soggy in wet conditions, wheezing through the air instead of flying properly. This last also meant that it was necessary to play in decent weather, and only the gentry could pick and choose when they would play. The poor man had to hope for a dry day when he had some leisure – which was not often – a further reason why the game was so little played by ordinary folk. It also explains why golf was played largely on the eastern side of Scotland, which is drier than the western side.

Though there is a general lack of detailed information about golf at the time, the seventeenth century has left us one remarkable and unique document, the first instruction pamphlet on how to play the game. It was written by one Thomas Kincaid in 1687. A courtier and general man-about-town in Edinburgh, Kincaid was clearly also a keen golfer. He took the trouble to write down his thoughts on how the game should be played and even summarized them in the form of a poem. His conclusions were simple and straightforward, and many of his ideas could with advantage be adopted by golfers today: 'In the swing you should maintain the same posture of the body throughout ... Turn the body as far to the left in the downswing as you have turned it to the right in the backswing ... The ball must be straight before your breast, a little towards the left foot.'

In the seventeenth century there were no Golf Clubs – associations of golfers formed to play the game among themselves, with premises on which to change their clothes and store their clubs and with well-defined, well-tended courses on which to play. These began to appear only in the latter half of the eighteenth century. Until then the game was played on rough seaside turf full of craters and natural bunkers and criss-crossed with cart tracks. There were no greens or tees, and the holes were rough-cut, becoming larger and rougher with the passage of time as players took sand from them to make

previous page:
(left) The Macdonald Boys, by Jeremiah Davison, rather artificially posed in the manner of the eighteenth century but giving us a good idea of red golfing coats.

(right) In the background to this 1784 portrait of William Inglis by David Allan can be seen the victory procession of the silver club. Inglis was Captain of the Honourable Company of Edinburgh Golfers from 1782 to 1784.

tees when driving off. Golf was played on seaside turf partly because the underlying sand allowed rapid drainage of water and partly because such grass is naturally short. There were no mowers then, and to play in long meadow grass would have meant a great many lost balls. Thus access to golf was limited not only by expense but also by the special terrain that it required and the difficulty of getting to it. When the term 'links' is used, as opposed to 'course', it refers to this terrain of short-grassed seaside turf, with underlying sand, on which golf was traditionally played.

There are no seventeenth-century wooden-headed clubs left and no authenticated iron clubs or feather balls. Nor are there any recorded rules of golf from that time. This does not mean that there *were* no rules, but players in each game probably came to a prior agreement about such matters. As there was no 'medal' play, arrangements for an individual match could be made but need not apply to other matches. Similarly there were no 'handicaps' other than, one assumes, arrangements to allow weaker players in a particular match to give the stronger ones a good game.

Like many absorbing pursuits golf can seem absurd to non-devotees. This lithograph of 1892, *The Delights of Golf – a Lost Ball*, pokes gentle fun at frustrated golfers, a perennial theme.

Tools of the Game

William Nicholson study, for R. Kipling *Almanack of Twelve Sports*, 1897-8.

Clubmaking early this century,
even in large numbers, was
'labour-intensive'. A view of
Robert Forgan's workshop, which
was sited opposite the 18th green
at St Andrews, shows hand-crafted
socket-head woods at several
stages of production.

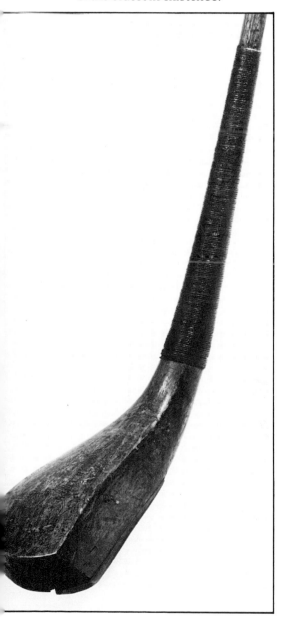

A 1790 spliced-head long-nosed wooden club by Simon Cossar, one of the oldest in existence.

The early records of golf obviously mean that there were clubmakers and ballmakers from the fifteenth century on. But as the number of golfers was small, and the eastern Scottish communities among whom the game was played had poor communications, there can have been few, if any, following the trade full-time for a living. Most golf clubs must have been made by enthusiastic local amateurs.

It was the taking up of golf by the King and his Court that gave rise to the trade of golf clubmaker. The Royal Court demanded a higher standard of clubs – and was prepared to pay for them.

Wooden Clubs

Until 1920 *all* golf clubs had wooden shafts, and the term 'wooden golf club' implies a club with a wooden head as well. Those who made wooden clubs were commonly known as clubmakers, and the earliest recorded one was a citizen of Perth whose main trade was that of a bower, or bowmaker. We do not know his name but we know that in 1502 James IV of Scotland purchased some 'golf clubbes' from him. At that time bowmaking was a common trade, and the fact that the clubs were ordered from a bowmaker rather than, say, one of the many carpenters or shipwrights suggests that he was chosen as a man who knew all about the elasticity and suppleness of various woods and so was in a better position to produce flexible, whippy clubs. But against this there are only two other references to bowmakers producing golf clubs. One was William Mayne, bowmaker, of Perth, from whom James VI of Scotland and I of England ordered clubs and whom he also appointed royal clubmaker. The other was William Fergie (1856-1924), of Archers' Hall, Edinburgh, Bowmaker to the Queen's Bodyguard and golf club- and ballmaker.

Other craftsmen with a special knowledge of the elastic properties of different woods were those who made fishing rods, and there is clear evidence that some of them also made golf clubs, though the written evidence all refers to the late nineteenth and early twentieth centuries.

In the eighteenth century we find many references to clubmakers, a number of them doubling as ballmakers. The Dickson family of Leith, near Edinburgh, were among the most prominent, their best recorded member being John Dickson, clubmaker. He died in 1787, but it is thought that earlier Dicksons were in the golf clubmaking trade. The first half of the century also

John Whyte Melville, of Bennochy and Strathkinness, famous golfer and for 67 years a member of the Royal and Ancient Golf Club. Uniquely he was twice elected Captain, but died before he could take office a second time. The portrait by Francis Grant was painted in 1874.

Scared-head old woods, from left: mid-spoon made by 'Old Tom' Morris; playclub by James McEwan; brassie by Willie Park Jun.; playclub by Robert Forgan – the plumes mark Forgan's status as the Prince of Wales' clubmaker; and playclub by Hugh Philp.

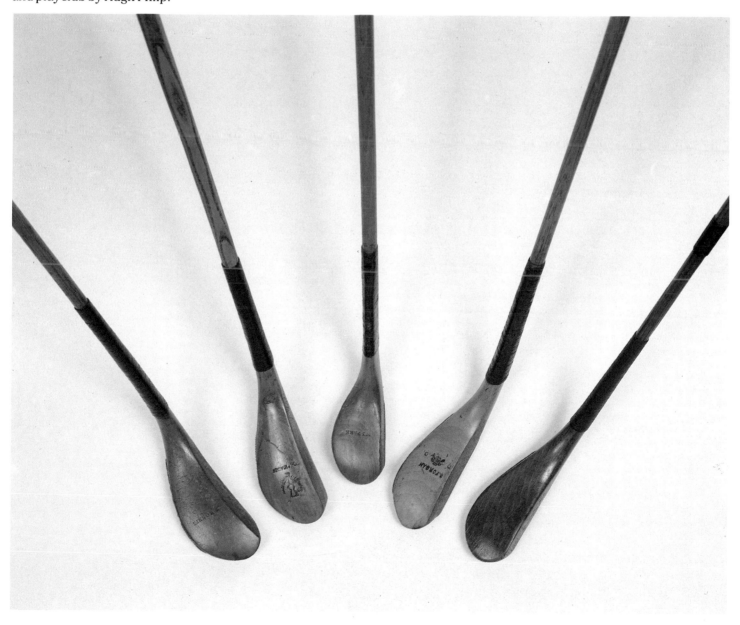

Victorian pros at St Andrews. In the centre, with his club aloft, is the great Allan Robertson, feather ballmaker and superb player. Note the pre-golf-bag caddies' armfuls of loose clubs.

records George and Henry Milne, club- and ballmakers, of St Andrews, and one David Dick of that town, but we know no more than that they plied the trade. A letter of 1735 refers to an Andrew Bailey then making clubs at Bruntsfield, Edinburgh, and later in the century a Thomas Comb also made clubs at Bruntsfield as well as running a local pub called the Foxtoun, which served as the Bruntsfield Clubhouse.

That there was a thriving Scottish trade in club- and ballmaking during the eighteenth century is shown by bills of lading at the Port of Leith, which record that between 1743 and 1751 some 168 clubs and nearly 1,000 balls were exported from there to South Carolina and Virginia. A later (1765) bill of lading at the port of Glasgow records the despatch of 18 golf clubs and 144 balls to Maryland. Unfortunately there is no indication of who made these exports but they do show that the trades of clubmaker and ballmaker were going concerns, and also prove conclusively that golf was being played in America some 130 years before its generally accepted starting time of 1880.

In 1770 Thomas Comb was followed at Bruntsfield by James McEwan, and Dickson was followed at Leith by Simon Cossar (1766-1811). McEwan and Cossar are significant, not only because theirs are the earliest authenticated wooden clubs still in existence but also because they bring us into the nineteenth century, which saw the flowering of the clubmaker's art.

The making of golf clubs during the first 70 years of the nineteenth century was largely in the hands of six families: the McEwans of Leith, and later of nearby Musselburgh; the Forgans of St Andrews; the Patricks of Leven, in Fife; the Morrises of St Andrews; the Parks of Musselburgh; and the Dunns of North Berwick. To these families must be added some individual clubmakers: Simon Cossar, of Leith, who preceded all of them; Hugh Philp (1782-1856), who preceded the Forgans at St Andrews and became a founder member of the Forgan family business after his daughter married into that family; and John Jackson (1805-78), of Perth.

These were the recognized master craftsmen of the trade, who entirely hand-made their clubs with the help of apprentices. In their heyday they produced incomparable clubs which are now prized collectors' items. But by the end of the century only the Patricks and the Forgans were still active. The master craftsmen had been ousted by mass production, which had become necessary to meet the demands of an ever-growing number of golfers.

A playclub and a short spoon used by Allan Robertson (1815-59), first player to break 80 at St Andrews.

Until 1900 the head of a wooden club was fixed to the shaft by means of a long splice, a 'scarffed' joint of the type long in use by shipwrights for repairing masts and spars. When clubmakers used it they called it a 'scared' joint, and clubs made in this way are commonly called 'scared head' clubs. The scared joint was held by glue and whipping, the latter usually of crude fisherman's twine. At the top of the shaft was the grip, which was of fine sheepskin and was thickened by having layers of cloth, known as 'listings', beneath it. Before 1820 the shafts of clubs were made of ash, but at about that date hickory from the southern part of the United States was introduced because of its superior steely whip. The club was protected from the weather by prolonged rubbing down with 'red keel', a substance whose composition is not now known and which was dropped from use after 1830, when varnish became available.

The clubs were several inches longer than modern ones, some 44-6 inches, and their feel was extremely whippy, with considerable torque. The heads were long (4-5 inches) and narrow (1½-2 inches). The face of the club was

Golf at Westward Ho!, 1882; the three Allan brothers – James (left), Matthew (putting) and John, the Club's professional, under the cool scrutiny of their caddies.

Osmond's 'Automatum', the first golf bag with legs forming a stand, was patented in 1893. The legs folded up when the bag was carried.

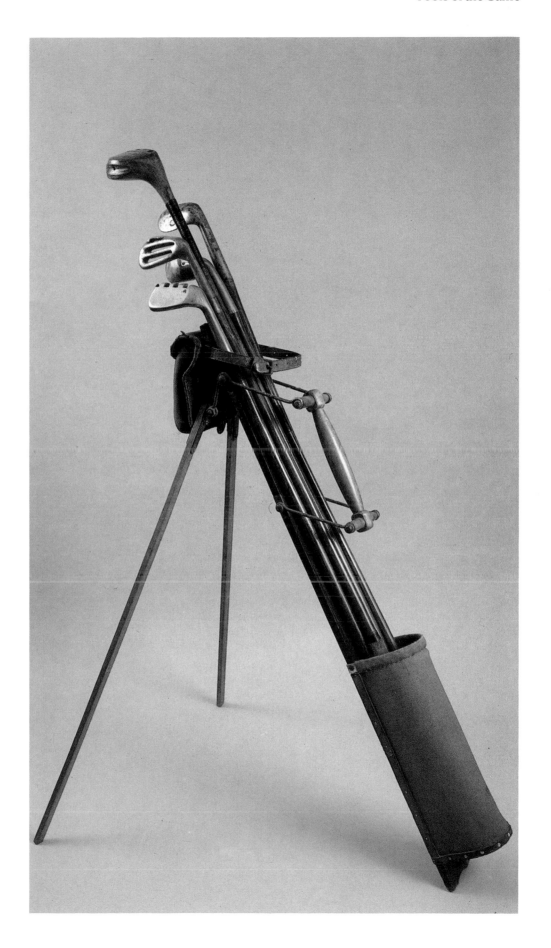

(left) A popular US songsheet, c.1910, hymned the praises of the caddie.

The Clubmaker's Craft

The ancient craft of golf clubmaking had no scientific rules; it was learnt by long apprenticeship and practice. In the very early days of golf it was taken up as a profitable sideline by bowmakers and fishing rod makers, whose skills with strong but supple woods lent themselves to it better than most. But as golf became more and more popular among the wealthy clubmaking emerged as a craft in its own right.

Nowadays, of course, there is a great industry mass-producing golf clubs of aluminium, steel, carbon fibre and other such twentieth-century materials, but there

1. Using a template to mark out a clubhead. The grain of the wood – usually beech or blackthorn – must run with the neck to avoid splitting on impact.

2. The head has been cut and shaped, and a cavity in it is filled with molten lead for added weight, judged by the clubmaker.

3. The leading edge of the club's 'sole' is recessed to take a strip of ram's horn, attached with glue and wood pegs.

is still a connoisseur's market for traditional wooden clubs – having both shaft and head of wood – and still a craftsman making them.

The pictures here show such clubs being made in the workshop of Mr Edward Davies at Northam, North Devon. As a teenage boy Mr Davies was apprenticed at Westward Ho! to the great clubmaker Charles Gibson, from North Berwick, himself a one-time apprentice – about 1875 – to the famous Tom Dunn. Mr Davies did not go on to become a clubmaker but spent his working life as a master carpenter in the shipbuilding yards at nearby Appledore. Yet he continued to make and repair golf clubs as a hobby, and when he retired from the shipyards he returned to his first love, making traditional wooden clubs with hickory shafts and spliced heads, using the skills he had learned some 50 years before.

Mr Davies is the last craftsman clubmaker in Britain, working in the honourable tradition founded by the early bow- and rodmakers.

5. The head and shaft spliced together, the joint is cleaned up on a rotary sander.

6. Jointed, and with lead and ram's horn in place, the club's 'whip' and 'loft' are gauged. Its whip can be increased by careful sanding. It then gets a final polish, whipping on the splice, a leather grip, its maker's name on its head, and is stained and varnished.

4. Neck and shaft are joined by a long splice. Here the neck half is being glued for assembly. The splice will be further strengthened with twine whipping.

only an inch deep and was gracefully curved, being 'turned in' at the toe, which made the face concave. Inserted into the leading edge of the club's sole, and held there by glue and three pegs, was a strip of ram's-horn ½-inch wide and ⅛-inch thick, whose purpose was to protect the wood and prevent its being chipped. When the horn eventually became damaged it could be removed and replaced with a new piece. This feature must be of great antiquity because no wooden club without it has ever been found. Clubs of this general type continued to be made until 1880.

During the first half of the nineteenth century a 'set' of golf clubs would be all wooden except for one iron. Wooden clubs – drivers or play clubs – were used for driving, and all shots through the green were effected with clubs such as long, middle and short spoons. These names referred to different lengths, but the clubs also had progressively increased loft. The putter was also of wood and was used for shots of up to 100 yards or even more. Essential for playing approach shots at this time was the 'baffing spoon', a club of great character used particularly for lofted shots. It got its name from the fact that in use it 'baffed' the ball, that is it struck the ground immediately behind it. As the club bounced off the ground it lifted the ball in the air. It was said to be a very pretty stroke in skilled hands but its length was difficult to control.

Another club much in use was the wooden niblick, much shorter in the head than other clubs and frequently equipped with a piece of brass on its sole to protect it from damage by stones. The wooden niblick was commonly used in any situation in which the longer-nosed clubs could not be made to 'sole' behind the ball, for example where the ball was in a tight 'cuppy' lie – in other words, lying in a slight small depression.

The solitary iron, which could easily burst a feather ball costing three times the price of the club itself, was used only for such desperate purposes as getting the ball out of bunkers, cart ruts or stony lies, situations in which a wooden head might disintegrate. When the new tough gutta-percha balls came into general use about 1850 iron clubs began to increase in numbers and wooden ones to decrease. This was not only because there was no danger of bursting the new balls. Lofted shots were found to be easier with iron clubs than with wooden ones, and the baffing spoon was relegated to the attic. Also, the hard new balls damaged the faces of wooden clubs, and clubs now cost more than balls.

In 1880 there came a change in the shape of club heads. They became much shorter (2-3½ inches) and wider (3-4 inches) but with deeper faces (1¼-1½ inches). But the most striking change was that the faces were now convex, bulging forward, so that they came to be called 'bulgers'. The new clubs were also shorter than earlier ones, with 40-to-42-inch shafts.

In 1900 a new wood for golf clubheads and a new way of fixing heads to shafts were introduced. Just as hickory from America had been found best for shafts, persimmon, a very hard wood, also American, was now found to be best for heads. Instead of fixing head to shaft by means of the long splice a hole was drilled in the head and the shaft's end inserted into it, in the same way that the shaft of an iron club was fitted into the head. The new clubs were called socket-headed clubs and the new method of fixing lent itself readily to machine production. American expertise came into play and by 1902 the US was exporting 100,000 golf clubs to Britain annually. The heads were rough finished, and the British professional had merely to polish them up and stamp his name on them. The craftsmen clubmakers were out of business.

(right) In *A St Nicholas Party* by Jan Steen, *c.*1670, a small boy holds up his Christmas present – a *colf* club and ball.

(below left) Two early blacksmith-made 'rutters', or rut-irons, with small heavy heads designed for playing balls out of the narrow cart tracks on rough links courses.

(below) This well-'dished' iron putting cleek belonged to Sir Hugh Lyon Playfair (1786-1861), a noted benefactor of the town and of the Golf Club of St Andrews.

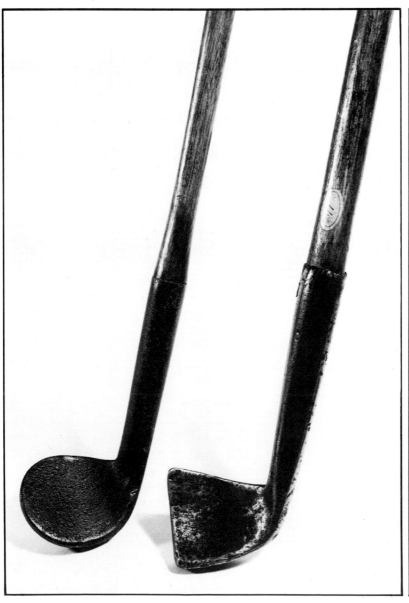

Iron Clubs

The old clubmakers were expert woodworkers but knew nothing of working metal. In the time of the feather ball few iron clubs were required and for those few the clubmakers got blacksmiths to make the metal heads and themselves fitted shafts of the right length and spring into the sockets.

Generally a blacksmith would make an iron clubhead by taking a straight piece of iron of the right thickness and cutting it to the length of the desired club face plus the length of the 'hosel', or socket. He would then heat one end of this piece and hammer it so that the thickness was halved. This part he then hammered round the tapered end of a piece of iron called a mandrel, making a tapered socket. The two edges of the metal that joined to form the socket were completely fused together so that no join line could be seen. This left the socket still in line with the face as one straight piece, so it was re-heated and, with the mandrel as a lever plus some further hammering, angled to the face by the right degree. A final procedure angled the face back, relative to the socket, to give it the right amount of loft. Such a blacksmith was an expert. If the line of fusion in a socket was visible he considered the head sub-standard and would probably sell it at the back door for a small sum to some keen player who would happily take it home and shaft it himself, thereby getting a cheap club.

When the clubmaker received the metal clubhead he drilled a hole through the upper part of the hosel to take the fixing rivet, then selected a shaft which his experience told him was suitable for the weight of the head and the club's purpose. He tapered the end of the shaft to fit tightly into the hosel, further securing it with glue and the rivet. For still more security the blacksmith would have made a series of indentations round the top of the hosel, giving it a sawtooth appearance, to improve its grip on the shaft. This indenting was called 'knopping', or 'knurling', and as the iron clubs were heavy it was large and crude as was the hosel itself.

The faces of early nineteenth-century clubheads were smooth and usually concave because wooden heads had always been shaped like that. They were also often concave in the other axis, rather like a hollow-ground razor blade. Whereas iron clubheads of the early nineeenth century, despite being crude and heavy, were in general appearance like modern-day clubs, those of the eighteenth century presented a bizarre appearance, for the clubhead had no 'toe', the end of the face being cut off vertically.

As the greater use of iron clubs quickly followed on the arrival, in 1848, of tough gutta-percha balls, and as golfers grew rapidly in number, blacksmiths skilled at making iron clubheads could make a living at it. Many smiths abandoned the other aspects of their trade and took up making clubheads full-time. At this stage the concave face was abandoned and the flat one was adopted.

An iron which had been available for some years and now became popular was the cleek, and from this the blacksmiths who specialized in making iron clubheads came to be known as 'cleekmakers'. The clubmaker was the man who made up a club from the iron head, and it was he who sold it, taking the credit and giving little to the cleekmaker. But as cleekmakers became more important they began asserting themselves by putting their own marks on the heads they made, so that most iron heads now had the clubmaker's name stamped on the back and the cleekmaker's mark in one corner. The marks were rather like the marks on pottery and porcelain, and they make interest-

Seven putters. From left: two wooden ones, *c*.1875; a wry neck blade putter, *c*.1920; a brass head putter, *c*.1895; another wooden one, *c*.1929; and two with aluminium heads, *c*.1929, *c*.1900. Willie Park Jun. invented the wry neck club. This one belonged to his daughter.

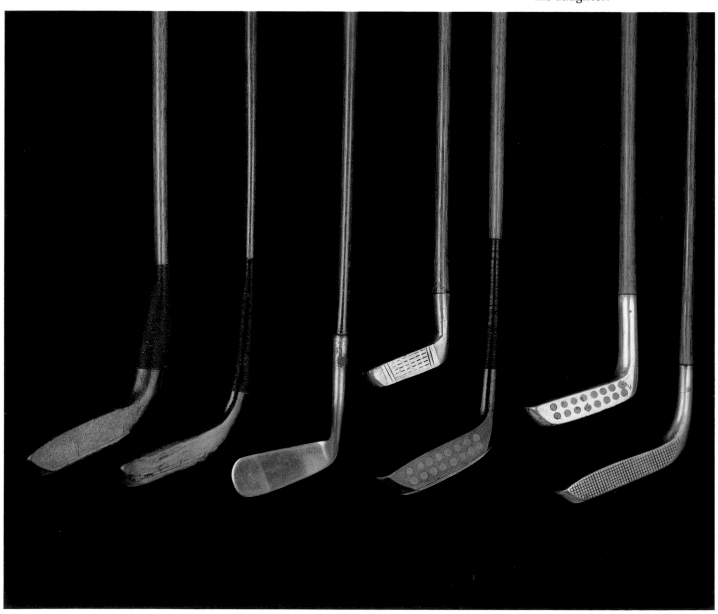

A collection of unusual and 'illegal' clubs on display at the Royal and Ancient Golf Club of St Andrews. Each of these was proscribed at some time because of the material used in its construction, or because of its shape and face markings. They include a driver made of compressed paper; a 'lipped' mashie and 'hollow-ground' sand wedge, made to give extra backspin; a Schenectady, and a centre-shafted putter made by Tom Morris; and several 'adjustable head' clubs, which, it was hoped, could replace a whole bagful.

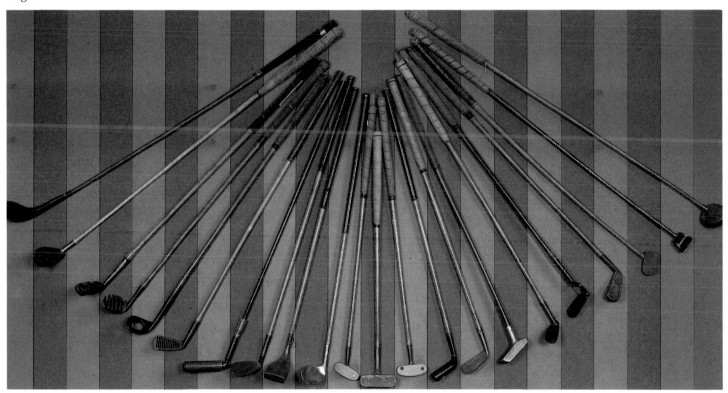

ing decorations on the iron clubs. Particular cleekmakers could be identified by such marks as pipes, anchors, crescent moons, crosses, diamonds, anvils, hearts, acorns, snakes, etc. Some famous early cleekmakers were: John Gray, in the Prestwick area; Carrick of Musselburgh; Wilson of St Andrews; Gourlay of Carnoustie; Condie of St Andrews; Anderson of Anstruther; Willie Park Junior of Musselburgh. By the end of World War I nearly all of these craftsmen had ceased trading. Of the later cleekmakers Gibson of Kinghorn and Spalding (who had come from America and set up in London) continued well into the 1930s by entering the mass production market.

Of the great variety of iron clubs eventually to be produced, all stemmed essentially from just three early forms: the rutter, the cleek and the lofter. The rutter, or rut-iron, evolved to meet the needs of early golfing, had a small head – not much bigger than a golf ball – and was usually heavy. It was for playing out of bunkers and, especially, cart ruts, a procedure for which the tiny head, which would fit into a narrow rut, made it invaluable. It was later to be modified into the niblick, which in turn was the forerunner of the pitching wedge and the sand wedge. The cleek was an iron with little loft and was used for long iron shots; it was the precursor of today's Nos. 1, 2 and 3 irons. The lofter had more loft than the cleek and was deeper faced; it was to lead to the mashie, which appeared in 1880, and the mashie-niblick. These clubs were the forerunners of all the irons now used to make approach shots – Nos. 4-8. The 'matched set' of irons did not appear until after World War I. By this time,

(right) Hand forging an iron head with ordinary blacksmith's tools.

An iron clubhead was made by beating a bar of iron flat, forming the wider part round a tapered 'mandrel' to make a socket, rounding the corners, then polishing up the whole.

The manufacture of golf
equipment is now a major
commercial industry. Modern golf
clubs are made using the latest
materials and technology, and
they are promoted and sold
through sophisticated advertising.

as has already been noted, the cleekmakers and clubmakers had been put out of business by the big mass production factories which turned out complete clubs.

By the end of World War I so many golf clubs were being made that the supply of good, properly seasoned hickory began to run out. But in the early 1920s, in the United States, a tubular steel golf club shaft was developed. It was an excellent shaft, and within a few years it had taken over from hickory, which virtually disappeared from clubmaking after the early 1930s. Steel shafts were used in iron and wooden clubs, and the irons were further improved by 1930 with heads of rustless chrome steel. The steel shaft and persimmon head formed the typical golf club until after World War II, when supplies of seasoned persimmon began to run out. Laminate wood heads came into use and are still used today, though some persimmon is still available.

In recent years further technical developments have produced shafts of carbon fibre (graphite), aluminium and other man-made materials, and clubheads of glass fibre, aluminium and so on have also been devised. All of these materials are still rather on trial, but doubtless one day a definitive 'new club', the answer to every golfer's prayer, will emerge, at least temporarily, until it is replaced by yet another real or imaginary 'breakthrough'.

The Golf Ball

As mentioned above, the early feather golf ball, or 'feathery', cost some three times as much as a golf club. This was because it took so much skill and time to make, a good ballmaker being able to produce perhaps three in a day. Furthermore such balls were easily damaged, so a golfer needed three or four to play.

The ball had an outer casing of bull's hide which had to be hand-stitched inside out, leaving unstitched only a slit some ¼-inch long. The casing next had to be turned 'outside in' through this tiny slit – no easy job – then stuffed with the boiled breast feathers of chickens or geese. The stuffing was done so tightly that more than an old-fashioned top-hatful of feathers was forced into the small ball – approximately the size of a modern golf ball – and in the later stages a long spike harnessed to the ballmaker's chest was used to exert maximum pressure. The slit was then closed with a single stitch and the ball was waterproofed with white lead paint.

Making such balls was a highly skilled trade requiring a long apprenticeship, and, as in early clubmaking, certain families became pre-eminent as ballmakers over several generations. Notable were the Dicksons of Leith, the Robertsons of St Andrews and the Gourlays of Musselburgh and Leith.

That the feather balls were good golf balls is shown by the fact that a drive of more than 300 yards with one is recorded. But they did not last long and they became soggy in wet conditions. And, as noted earlier, the prohibitive cost of the balls meant that only the wealthy could afford to play. Then, in 1848, the properties of gutta-percha became known.

Gutta-percha is a resin derived from a tree found in Malaya (now Malaysia). By judicious cutting of the tree's bark the resin can be made to exude from it. The resin sets and becomes hard, but it will readily soften again if immersed in hot water, when it can be shaped by hand or in a mould, then allowed to cool and harden in its new shape. It was soon realized that this material could be shaped into golf balls. The resulting balls were able to take a great deal of

A mashie niblick, *c.*1910, forerunner of today's No. 9 iron. This is a 'Ted Ray' model with hand-punched face.

(below) A modern club. Veteran Gene Sarazen used this No. 5 iron to hole in one in the 1973 Open at Troon.

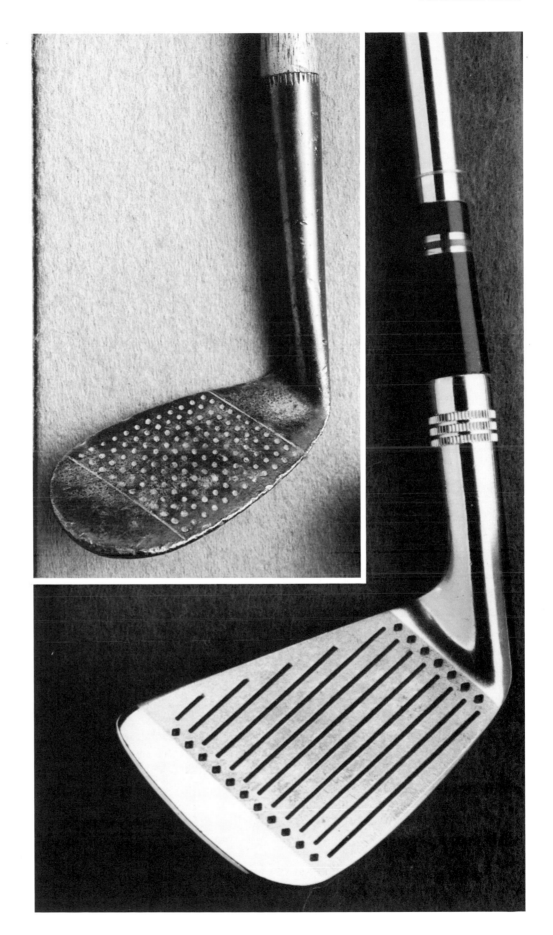

Men's Fashion on the Fairways

In the early days golfers played in their everyday clothes. Those of the aristocracy may be seen in the *Grand Match* (p. 90) and of the labouring men in the essay on the Morrises (p. 108). But all golfers would have worn hob-nailed boots, and during the nineteenth century the wealthier players sought more practical golf clothing. Eventually they adopted knickerbockers and the Norfolk jacket. The latter, designed to give grouse-shooting men free shoulder movement, proved ideal for golf. In summer the same golfers would play in a cricketing costume of blazer, white flannels and canvas shoes.

Many who played over public ground, wore highly visible red coats to alert the public to the hazard of flying golf balls. When golf came to be played only on Club courses and such warnings were no longer needed the red coat was refined into a sort of mess jacket for wear at Club dinners and other such formal occasions.

1. This reproduction from a mid-'20s advertisement shows the classic plus fours and pullover of the time – also the popular stereotypes of frustrated golfer and cynical caddy.

2. Turn-of-the-century Norfolk jacket and knickerbockers, worn by A. H. Hilton.

3. For the fifties' golfer – pullover, roomy slacks and shady cap.

4. Pro golfer Rodger Davis sports plus twos, a sweater and some fancy stockings.

50

5. HRH the Prince
of Wales carrying
on the Royal golf
connection c.
1924.

51

James Mentiply, the foreman at Forgan's at the turn of the century. Traditionally a top-hatful of feathers went into one of the old feather balls. In fact a lot more were forced in.

A display of gutta-percha golf balls made by Andrew Forgan.

punishment, were impervious to wet and were much cheaper to make than the old feather balls. Suddenly golf was within the reach of the many. There was a dramatic growth in the number of golfers. Because the new balls – called 'guttas' – could take so much punishment more iron play was possible. Indeed it was found that gutta-percha balls which had sustained some cuts and scars flew better than smooth new ones, and it quickly became the practice of the makers to give them a textured surface. At first this was done by hand with the sharpened end of a tack hammer, but soon the textured pattern was embodied in the mould.

The situation had now changed. Balls were cheap and tough, excellent for iron play but liable to damage wooden club faces, which came increasingly to be made – or repaired – with animal horn or vulcanite inserts. The ball was now half the price of the club. Because of the nature of gutta-percha and the readiness with which it could be made into balls it was easy to devise mass production methods which made them even cheaper. Toward the end of the

Early gutta-percha balls (bottom left) were hand-moulded, then hammered to give them texture. Later came individual patterned moulds (right), then machine-moulded balls (centre).

(left) A collection of golf balls, including a wooden ball (left), a 'feathery' (centre), and a smooth unpainted gutta (right). The red ball is for playing in snow.

(right) Feather ballmaking equipment. The leather-holder (left) was used during stitching and stuffing. The two long awls with chest pieces (centre) allowed maximum pressure when stuffing. The small implements are starting stuffers and calipers for checking the ball's size.

(below) An elegant nineteenth-century beechwood clubhead and 'feathery' ball.

century chemical additives made the gutta-percha balls fly better; they also became even tougher and more destructive of wooden club faces.

In 1900 the world of golf again became indebted to the United States, for in Akron, Ohio, there was invented an even better golf ball than the gutty, as the new composition gutta balls were called. It was made of rubber in the form of a narrow strip of great length wound tightly round a central core, the whole being then encased in a gutta-percha covering. The brainchild of Coburn Haskell, it was called a 'Haskell', though others, such as John Gammeter, had more to do with its production. The new ball was as durable as the gutty but softer, so it did not damage club faces. And though a little more expensive than the gutty it was much easier to use, which more than outweighed the extra expense.

The Haskell method of making a golf ball, with minor improvements, is still the commonest method in use, though recently solid balls have appeared and are increasingly being used.

(right) An advertisement for the 'Haskell' golf ball, patented in 1899 and made of tightly wound rubber encased in gutta-percha.

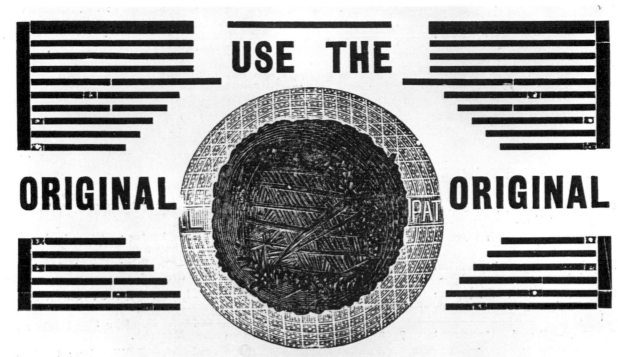

Allen E. Sealy 1893

Expatriate nineteenth-century British golf-lovers established a Club at Pau, in the Pyrenean foothills, where they went for the winter. The first golf course on the Continent of Europe, Pau is seen here as painted by Allen E. Sealy in 1892.

The Golfing Explosion

William Nicholson lithograph, from R. Kipling *Almanack of Twelve Sports*, 1897-8.

(left) The golf course as marriage market. A cartoon of 1895 from the *Illustrated London News* sees golf in terms of eligible bachelors, marriageable girls and approving dowagers.

A rare Royal Doulton bowl depicting men in Stuart dress playing golf.

From the mid-eighteenth century golf went through a period of doldrums. Neither George III, William IV nor the young Queen Victoria evinced any interest in it and it ceased to be a Court game. People of lower income groups could not afford to play, and despite the keenness of those who loved golf the number of players dwindled as the enthusiasts grew too old or infirm to play without being replaced by new recruits.

Golf might well have ceased altogether and died out, as *colf* had vanished from Holland, had it not been for the Freemasons. Their enthusiasm and organizing ability sustained the game and developed it in healthy continuity for about 100 years, from 1750 to 1850. It is very doubtful that golf was their main diversion at the beginning. Wining, dining, ritual, speechmaking, good fellowship and the excitement of a wager were their principal concerns. Golf was the means of working up an appetite, the occasion for having a bet or two and generally preparing oneself for a large meal accompanied by generous quantities of wine and spirits.

Indeed, in the early days of golfing associations wining and dining took clear precedence over playing golf. There is plenty of evidence of this, but a few examples will make the point. In his most ably compiled history of the North Berwick Golf Club (*In the Wind's Eye*), Alistair Adamson states that the Club's carefully kept records show clearly the at least equal emphasis accorded to dining and golfing. At the North Berwick's first meeting, in 1832, there was a 'competition in mutton' between two members. The minutes of the meeting devote ten words to golf, then go into extensive details of the menu and dinner arrangements for the next meeting. These were that Sir David Baird was to produce mutton, Mr Anderson pickled pork, Campbell and Clanranald six bottles of whisky and Captain Brown a haggis. Sir David also promised three dozen bottles of champagne. The dinner was consumed by 27 people.

In the following year Baird again undertook to produce mutton, Mr Sligo a lamb, Mr Anderson a pig, the Secretary a turbot, Mr Craigie a salmon, Mr Campbell a dozen bottles of whisky and Clanranald a further dozen of whisky.

At Leith the Company of Gentlemen Golfers held regular dinners at which wagers were placed and were recorded in a Bets Book – and by no means all the bets were on golf. In 1801 14 dining members are recorded as having paid for large quantities of drink at a dinner, including port, ale and spruce, gin and

(right) William St Clair of Roslin, who founded the first Golf Club in 1744, seen here in the uniform of the Gentlemen Golfers, later the Honourable Company of Edinburgh Golfers. The portrait was painted by Sir George Chalmers in 1771 and now hangs in the Royal Company of Archers' Hall, Edinburgh.

Presentation of the Silver Club at a ceremonial dinner at the Muirfield Clubhouse of the Honourable Company of Edinburgh Golfers. The company moved its Golf Club to Muirfield *c.*1890.

Schoenhut's American 'parlour golf' game of the 1930s. The figure on the left is operated by a lever in the handle. Various clubs can be attached.

brandy, sherry (seven bottles), claret (16 bottles), and rum and toddy. All this alcohol preceded and accompanied a very large meal.

At Blackheath dinners have been regularly held – and a Bets Book kept – since 1797, again the bets not all relating to golf.

Wining and dining were important ceremonial occasions at which the members were required to wear uniform. Failure to do so, or the commission of some other minor infringement such as speaking out of turn, could give rise to a 'fine'. The commonest of these was being sentenced to drink a gallon of claret. Those were times, before Phylloxera had struck the vineyards, when it was customary to drink claret of the current year, usually from one-pint silver tankards. The minutes of early nineteenth-century Golf Clubs read like menu cards.

It may surprise many that the Freemasons played such an important role in early golf, but this is simply because as a secret society they kept quiet about it. In recent years much evidence has been discovered of their involvement in late eighteenth- and nineteenth-century golf, and detailed accounts are to be found in such books as *Royal Blackheath*, *Golf in the Making* and *The Compleat Golfer*, but a brief one is given here.

The foundation stone of the Clubhouse of the Company of Gentlemen Golfers was laid by William St Clair of Roslin in the presence of the company's whole committee. The recorded account of the ceremony names all the committee members and gives their Masonic status. St Clair of Roslin was the Hereditary Grand Master Mason of Scotland and all but two of the other committee members are listed as Master Masons.

The Knuckle Club was a club within the Blackheath Club, with its own separate dinners and meetings at which fines were imposed for non-attendance, not wearing Club uniform and so on. New members are recorded as having 'gone through the ordeal bravely'. They drank toasts, especially the 'three times three', a typical Masonic toast. Would-be members could be blackballed, a procedure, also typically Masonic, that worked as follows. Members called on to vote on the worthiness of a man to become a new member did so by putting a ball into an opening in an otherwise closed box. Each member could secretly insert either a white ball or a black one. The white indicated approval, the black disapproval, and one black ball in the box was enough to bar the aspirant from membership. He would not be entitled to an explana-

A Royal Doulton Plate celebrating the 'nineteenth hole', traditional golfers' euphemism for the Club bar.

(right) Some American and English board games with golfing themes.

(left) Detail depicting a game of golf, from a Chinese famille-rose punch bowl (below).

THE "CHAD VALLEY" GAMES   MADE AT HARBORNE, ENGLAND.

GOLFING

THE GREAT
INDOOR GOLF GAME.

INVENTED BY Sir Frederick Frankland, Bart.   COPYRIGHT RESERVED.

The Game of Golf

MANUFACTURED BY J. H. SINGER, NEW YORK, U.S.A.

Tinplate mechanical golfing games of the 1920s and 1930s.

tion for his rejection, nor would anyone know who had blackballed him – except the blackballer. This method of voting on new members is still used by some Clubs but no longer has any connection with the Freemasons, though they began it.

The Masonic connection is clear too from the records of the Royal Burgess Golfing Society of Edinburgh, whose captain was allowed to elect three new members a year 'on the shake of a hand' and whose members agreed at one time to purchase three dozen aprons, part of the Masons' uniform. The records also refer to new members 'going through the ordeal bravely' and giving all the right answers.

As parts of a secret society, if these Clubs ever broke up or disbanded they destroyed all minutes and records, and a common tale among the older Golf Clubs with Masonic origins was that there had been a disastrous fire which had unfortunately destroyed their precious documents. Closer examination often reveals no real evidence of a fire. When the Knuckle Club was disbanded its few remaining members agreed to 'meet as ordinary members' in future and to destroy the Club's records, though some documents escaped destruction.

The usual reasons for disbanding a Club were either or both of two: the number of golfing Freemasons in a locality might have dwindled to a point at which there were too few for the Club to be worth carrying on or, more commonly, a growing number of Club members were enthusiastic golfers but not Freemasons, and this made it difficult for the Club to continue as a Masonic lodge. This latter state of affairs became prevalent about 1850, when the cheaper golf ball and the increased leisure of workers due to industrial developments brought thousands more golfers on to the turf.

These pages imply no criticism of the Freemasons. Given that they were a secret society and must remain so, praise is due to them for keeping the game alive and bringing the benefits of properly organized Clubs, keen and fair competitions and formal rules of play to a game which had hitherto been played pretty haphazardly. For though the Masons started playing golf as an adjunct to having bets and as a means of working up an appetite it was not long before they were bitten by the allure of the game itself and became keen players.

As noted above, the Masons were fond of ceremony and uniforms, their

Items of Coalport china – a water jug, a teapot and a three-handled mug – decorated with golfing figures.

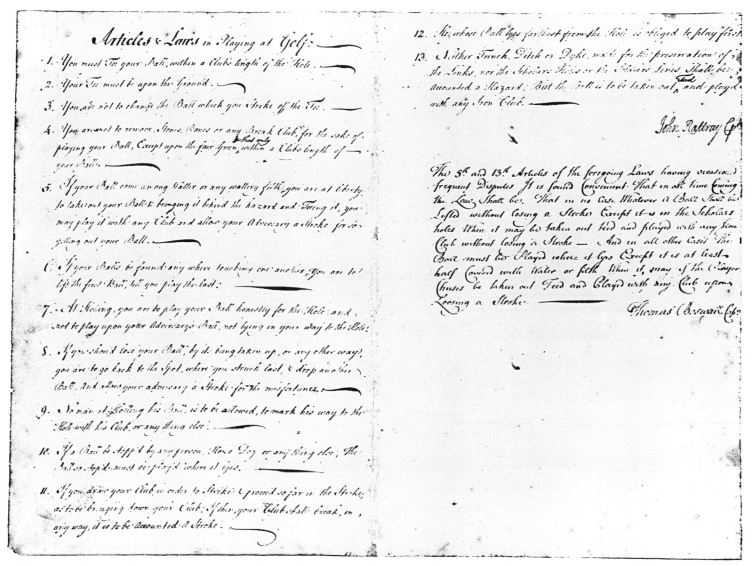

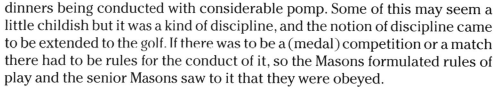

The first rules of golf, drawn up at Leith in 1744 by the Company of Gentlemen Golfers and signed by their Captain, John Rattray, first winner of the Silver Club.

dinners being conducted with considerable pomp. Some of this may seem a little childish but it was a kind of discipline, and the notion of discipline came to be extended to the golf. If there was to be a (medal) competition or a match there had to be rules for the conduct of it, so the Masons formulated rules of play and the senior Masons saw to it that they were obeyed.

In 1744 the Golf Club of the Company of Gentlemen Golfers, later known as the Honourable Company of Edinburgh Golfers, was founded at Leith. Though St Andrews is known as the home of golf, Leith is in fact the birthplace of *organized* golf and the concept of the Golf Club. As Edinburgh's port, Leith was conveniently close to the city. Unfortunately the land there was not the best on which to play golf. Members often played on the true links course at Musselburgh, a few miles down the coast, and in later years the Club moved there. They would also sail across the Forth of Firth from Leith to the Fife coast, then take a coach to St Andrews, whose links they found particularly good for golf and where they could also meet other golfers to play with.

When the St Andrews Club was established ten years later the new Club called for support from the Gentlemen Golfers, who readily gave it, as the two Clubs had many members in common and they were all brother Masons. These dates do not imply that golf was first played at those times in

(left) Some of these early books on golf are very valuable and collectable in their own right. The game now has an enormous literature.

St Andrews October Meeting, painted by Thomas Hodge in 1862.

those places; they refer to the start of properly organized and constituted Golf Clubs, with premises where members could change their clothes, keep their clubs and have a meal and a drink after a game. The older, less formal kinds of golf had probably been played in both localities for hundreds of years before.

The Clubs also arranged competitions and formulated rules of play, but they accepted the concepts of sportsmanship and fair play, with the consequence that there were only 13 rules – easily listed on one side of a sheet of paper – a happy contrast with today's 34 rules plus a vast number of subsections, the whole filling a 73-page book. The first formal rules of golf were established at Leith in 1744. When the St Andrews Club was formed the members laid down their own rules of play, but these differed scarcely at all from those at Leith.

It was at St Andrews that the 18-hole course evolved. The area of the links was long and narrow, and conveniently made nine holes going out to the end. On the way back along the links golfers played to the same nine greens, those playing back being given priority over those playing out. Later, as more people took up golf, the greens were made larger, each with a second hole. One half of a green was used by those playing the first nine holes while those playing the second nine used the other. Other early golf courses had five, seven, nine or 22 holes, depending on the size and shape of the links, but eventually it was established by the Royal and Ancient Club of St Andrews that 18 holes should be adopted on all courses.

The Masonic lodges had a good communications network, and the first rules of golf, formulated at Leith, were quickly on the grapevine to all other Masonic Clubs, such as Perth, Blackheath and so on. Consequently all of the early Golf Clubs had the same rules of play except for some variations to allow for local conditions. A good example of cross-membership is one Andrew Duncan, Master Mason, who was a Founder Committee member of the Honourable Company of Edinburgh Golfers as well as, at different times, Captain of St Andrews and Captain of Blackheath.

So the Freemasons introduced Golf Clubs, formulated rules of play and kept the game going through the difficult years. But they did more than that.

A tournament at Leith in 1867. Note the absence of special dress. Golf was usually played in everyday clothes.

Muirfield Clubhouse. If golf has a distinctive architecture it seems to owe much to the design of cricket pavilions. The very early clubhouses were wooden huts or tents. Today's rival the best country clubs.

They used their considerable influence to spread the game beyond the shores of Britain. Scottish golfing enthusiasts, sent by the great business houses of London or by the Colonial Service to every part of the Empire and to other countries, took the game and their love of it with them. In 1830 a Golf Club was started in Calcutta; in 1842 one was founded in Bombay, as was another in New South Wales; between 1810 and 1860 Clubs came into being on various islands of the West Indies; in 1873 Montreal got its first Golf Club. Meanwhile, about 1860, the first Golf Club on the Continent of Europe was founded by British enthusiasts at Pau, in the foothills of the French Pyrenees.

Probably because most of these golfing travellers were sent from London, the great centre of business and Government, their Masonic brothers at Blackheath had close connections with all of them. The Calcutta Club was particularly closely associated with Blackheath, and indeed still sends its annual Club minutes to the London parent Club. Blackheath presented trophies to its overseas brothers and the overseas Clubs sent trophies – and other presents – to Blackheath. When a Captain of the New South Wales Club became a father he informed Blackheath and sent them a present, at which Blackheath made him an honorary member and its members toasted the infant.

Perhaps, with hindsight, the Freemasons' most important effort in encouraging the spread of golf overseas was in introducing the game into America. In 1743 David Deas of Charleston, South Carolina, the first Provincial Grand Master Mason in the United States, ordered from Scotland 96 golf clubs and 432 balls. They were sent to him from the port of Leith, where a bill of lading exists as evidence of the order, the date of shipment, the destination and the name of the consignee. Deas and his brother were from Leith, and would have learnt their golf there. Other shipments, from Glasgow to Virginia in 1750 and 1751, account for a further 72 golf clubs and 576 balls, and in 1765 18 clubs and 144 balls went from Glasgow to Maryland. The consignees for these are not known, but it is very unlikely that such quantities of clubs and very expensive balls were to be used by one individual. In the case of the Deas brothers the clubs and balls were certainly destined to equip a Golf Club at Charleston, and in view of David Deas' Masonic status the Club would doubtless have been a Masonic lodge. It is interesting that the Charleston Club is of an earlier date than the Honourable Company, but unfortunately – true to

(right) Olive trees and Roman ruins enhance the cover of a 1931 brochure inviting golfers to holiday in Italy.

Early English golf. F. P. Hopkins' 1880 painting of Westward Ho! shows the tin hut then serving as a Clubhouse. Behind it is the 'Pebble Ridge' of rocks that prevent the Atlantic flooding the links.

Masonic tradition – the Club minutes were 'lost' at some point in later years so we know nothing of its activities. The number of balls and clubs despatched to Virginia and Maryland suggest that these too were for Clubs rather than individuals.

The Masons equipped their Clubhouses and decorated their dinner tables in a manner compatible with their love of pomp and ceremony. On the walls hung portraits of the Captains; members drank from silver tankards and presented claret jugs, decanters and silver ornaments to grace the dinner table; medals were struck for the winners of competitions; gold and silver cups were presented. The Honourable Company, Blackheath and the Royal and Ancient Golf Club of St Andrews managed to persuade their local Town Councils to present silver clubs to be played for annually, each winner to affix to the club a silver ball with his name inscribed on it. In addition the names of captains, Presidents and the winners of major competitions were not only entered in Club records but were inscribed on Honours Boards that were hung on the Club walls.

Leading Masons encouraged Club members to honour the game of golf, gave gifts to their Clubs, commissioned portraits of their more worthy brethren, sang songs in praise of the game and wrote about it. They supported the playing of golf in a fair and sportsmanlike manner so that only the previously mentioned 13 rules were necessary. Decisions not covered by these rules were made 'in the spirit of the game', a notion not easily defined in words but readily understood by those with golf's true interests at heart.

Golfers owe the Masons a debt of gratitude that would have been acknowledged long ago had it not been that the essentially secret nature of Freemasonry caused them to destroy their records and cover their tracks so cleverly. In the event it has taken 150 years for their invaluable contribution to golf to be recognized.

The advent of the gutta-percha golf ball, offering cheaper golf, came at the height of the Industrial Revolution, when the artisan class was enjoying more leisure and more money to spend. Thus golf ceased to be a pursuit solely for Masons and the well-heeled and was taken up by thousands of 'ordinary' British people. Another factor in the golf explosion was the fast-developing railways, which made it easier and cheaper to get about the country so that many more golfers could now play not only on their local courses but on

'Old Tom' Morris quenches his thirst at the 'ginger beer hole', the 4th at St Andrews, where David 'Old Da' Anderson, retired caddie and green-keeper, sold the beverage.

The Honourable Company of Edinburgh Golfers played an annual Silver Club tournament. Winners' names were inscribed on silver golf balls, which were attached to the club, here being ceremoniously paraded.

D. Allan. 1787.

others far afield. Another element was the invention of the mower. Before that inland golf was not really possible, for grass grew so long in summer that balls were easily lost and play was practicable in an ordinary meadow only in early spring or late summer.

There were now more golf courses in Scotland, but in England the progress in the late nineteenth century from a single course in 1864 was truly an explosion.

Growth of Societies and Golf Clubs in the United Kingdom

1800	1870	1890	1900	1910
7	34	387	2330	4135

The effect of the railways on the habits and movements of golfers may be seen in the records of a nineteenth-century annual golfing pilgrimage. In the late 1860s Blackheath members formed a regular habit of attending the Spring and Autumn Meetings at Westward Ho!, at that time the only true links outside of Scotland. From there both Blackheath and Westward Ho! members entrained for Liverpool to play in the Spring and Autumn Meetings at Hoylake, the even newer links of the Royal Liverpool Golf Club. Also playing at Hoylake were golfers who had come south from Prestwick, St Andrews, Muir-

Ladies' golf at Westward Ho!, 1880,
recorded by F. P. Hopkins. The
Clubhouse was a white silk tent,
erected for the day, and male
associate members of the Ladies'
Club acted as markers in
competitions. Westward Ho! was
one of the first Clubs where
women could play proper golf.

The railways facilitated travel to and from the increasing number of golf courses around the country. This poster by John Hassall seeks to persuade golfers of the attractions of the east coast.

GREAT EASTERN RAILWAY

THE EAST COAST.
IDEAL FOR GOLFING.

Ladies' Fashion on the Fairways

1. Lisalotta Neumann wears the comfortable loose clothes that are fashionable today.

2. Victorian golfers at Portrush wearing boaters and long skirts.

Female incursions into golf were stoutly resisted by the men, and even when a Ladies' Club was allowed at St Andrews in 1867 its members were forbidden the links and confined to putting. Early women's golf was a painfully genteel affair. To show an ankle was indelicate; to show concentration was – perhaps worse – 'unwomanly'.

A further handicap was the feminine clothing of the day. Bustles, full-length skirts, bonnets and corsets – the last *de rigeur* for any true lady – were not ideal golfing garb. Voluminous skirts billowed out on windy days, obscuring the ball, and women golfers took to wearing elastic bands round their waists, to be pushed down to knee level when the wind blew, to control the skirt.

After World War I women's golf dress became much freer. A cloche or beret replaced the bonnet and a blouse or cardigan was worn with a calf-length tweed skirt and purpose-made golf shoes. Yet even by 1920 there were still women who played at golf, concerned more with fashion than with the game and often appearing on the greens in elegant ensembles not calculated to help their swings.

By the 1940s the costume, while remaining feminine, had become very practical, allowing a free swing. Hats were abandoned except on wet or windy days, and sweaters or cardigans were worn with knee-length skirts, 'sensible' stockings and spiked golf shoes. Today's trousered women (left) have really achieved parity with the men and, finally, compare the brief shorts, shirt and sun visor seen opposite with the bustles and bonnets pictured above.

3. Latest British fashions in wool – a golf sweater in Alpaca worn with a checked tweed skirt, 1947.

4. The foibles of ladies sometimes provoke censure (from the course at La Napoule, France, 1927).

5. The first trousered lady championship contender – Gloria Minoprio, 1934. She also used only one club.

6. The Minimalist: today's golfers follow the sun – and dress accordingly.

7. A '20s cloche and cardigan.

8. *Bon ton* on the fairway, 1924· sketch from an advertisement for a knitted sports coat on sale from Debenham and Freebody for 39/6 (*c.£2*).

9. A shady hat and stylish suit, worn in Monte Carlo, 1921.

10. Bonnets and bunkers: genteel golfing ladies at St Andrews.

Dear, charming Ladies! Please do not wear shoes with high heels or–I am sorry–I shall have to saw them off, as they make too many holes on our greens, and one is quite enough.

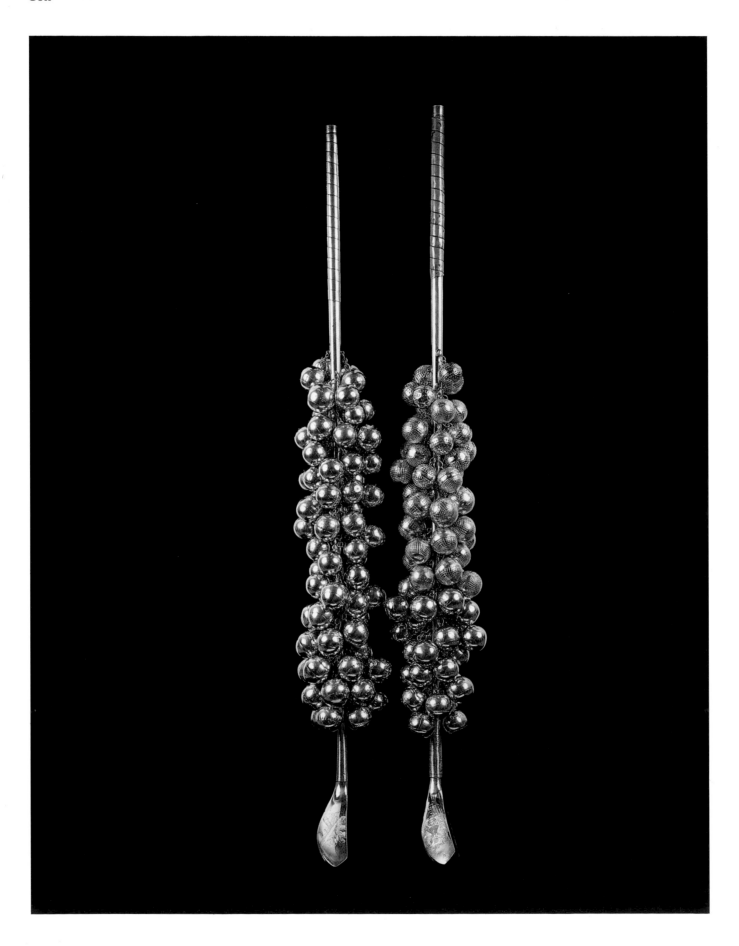

(left) The Captain's Silver Club and
Balls, 1754 (left) and 1819 (right),
from St Andrews.

Stylized golfing figures were
popular with 1920s practitioners
of art deco. These brooches are
typical.

field and other Clubs. At the end of the Hoylake meeting the whole company of golfers went north by rail to play in the Spring and Autumn Meeting at St Andrews. This annual migration was made possible by rail travel and the careful arrangement of Club dates.

For some years women had been playing a sort of golf of their own that was little more than genteel putting. But in 1868 they began to play 'proper' golf, and their arrival on the golfing scene produced a considerable swelling of the numbers of golfers. Male golfers, true to Masonic tradition, frowned on the whole idea and offered the women scant encouragement. Only at Westward Ho! were they truly welcomed. There they had their own links and, later, their own professional. Male members of Westward Ho! – who had originally suggested the separate Ladies' Club – were made associate members and acted as 'markers' on medal days. A member of the men's Club presented the ladies with a gold medal to play for. It may be significant that Westward Ho!, the Royal North Devon Golf Club, is the oldest Club in which no evidence of Masonic activities can be found. By contrast, at St Andrews ladies played at putting but were not allowed on the men's links. Nevertheless they had arrived and were to stay. A Ladies' Championship was instituted in 1893 and by 1899 there were 128 ladies' Golf Clubs in the United Kingdom.

If the late nineteenth-century growth of golf in Britain may be called an explosion then the later growth of the game in America must be described as volcanic. In 1888 there were about 10 golfers in the United States; in 1946 there were five million, who were said to be buying 30 million golf balls annually and spending $75 million a year on equipment. Today those figures can be multiplied many times over.

There has been equally remarkable growth in other countries since World War II, and it is a reasonable estimate that there are now some 50 million golfers throughout the world. The Japanese have taken to the game in large numbers, but they have few golf courses, and organized Japanese golf expeditions to many parts of the world are now common and increasing.

Golf is now a sports colossus supported and encouraged by a multi-billion-dollar industry that produces magazines telling golfers how to play, what current golfing heroes are doing, what is happening in women's golf – both amateur and professional – the whole lavishly accompanied by advertisements for every imaginable kind of golfing accessory – clubs, balls, tees, clothing, anything that can be connected, however remotely, with golf. There is a never-ending variety of 'new' clubs that are supposed to improve your stroke, new balls that are supposed to fly farther, improved golf bags, trolleys, carts and caddy cars, gadgets for practising golf at the office, in the home, in the car, even on the moon, for nowhere in the Universe is out of bounds to the dedicated golfer. Add to all this the instructional books, films, videos, biographies of the champions... The list is endless as millions of golfers aspire to emulate their heroes and heroines and improve their own games.

Ladies' golf offered new scope to artists of fashion. This beauty's follow-through may be a little languid but she represents golfing *bon ton* of the early 1900s (artist unknown).

(left, above) An art deco cigarette lighter, *c.*1920, features a lady golfer.

(left) Graceful ladies play a somewhat Arcadian version of golf on a decorative pocket watch, *c.*1900.

Many advertisers have used golfing themes. Bovril's lassie, in a feminine version of the classic red coat and a sensible skirt-length, looks at ease with her club.

(left) Early 1920s Royal Doulton china decorated with golfing figures in a mock Tudor costume made popular by a 'Rules of Golf' series advertising Perrier Water.

The Golfing Humorist

1. Unexpected hazards feature in many golf jokes. Print from Crombie's *Rules of Golf*.

2. Lost balls and apoplexy are of the essence.

3. The fanatic gets in a few strokes on any excuse.

4. A specious argument against ladies' golf adduced by the humorist Lawson Wood.

Though golfers take their game very seriously it can have its comic aspects, in its possibilities of minor disaster, chagrin, discomfiture and frustration. Nevertheless, few comedians have made a joke of golf, perhaps because many play the game themselves and share other players' reverence for it. Typical examples of this are Bob Hope and Bing Crosby, both keen players, who made many humorous films but seldom introduced the funny side of golf into them.

The late W. C. Fields made a number of short films on golf, characterized by the shamelessly outsize putter, the handful of change tactically rattled as an opponent is about to play, the ball slyly substituted in the rough or holed with a discreet kick. Of full-length comedy films, only one comes to mind – *Green Grass Widows* – made in Hollywood in the 1920s and co-starring two US professionals, Walter Hagen and Leo Diegel.

For the most part the funny side of golf seems to have been left to the cartoonists, doubtless an irreverent breed of men who do not realize what a serious matter it is! *Punch* published its first golf cartoon in 1886, thereby founding a tradition that placed golfers among the pantheon of comic stereotypes.

IN CONFERENCE

5. The hushed solemnity of a crucial putt seems comic – to others.

THE MAN WHO MISSED THE BALL ON THE FIRST TEE AT ST. ANDREWS.

6. H. M. Bateman's sketch makes fun of the nightmare possibilities when driving off from the first tee at St Andrews before a large crowd. After this one there's only the revolver in the study.

The Grand Match, painted *c*.1850 by Charles Lees of the Royal Scottish Academy,
conveys the tension as golfing gentry putt for the last hole.

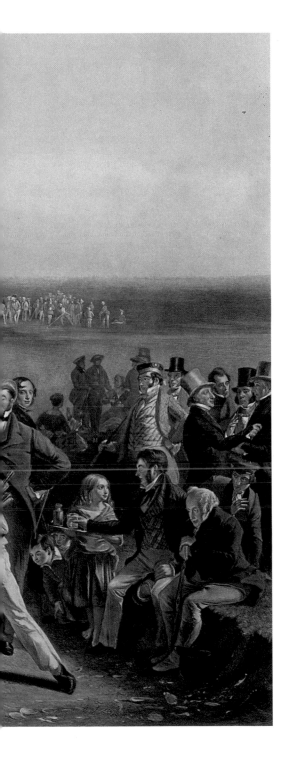

Tournament Golf

Arthur Rackham engraving, from R. H. Lyttelton *Outdoor Games, Cricket and Golf*, 1901.

This 1858 photograph of a
tournament at St Andrews shows
the rough quality of the 18th
green. One of the cannons in the
background would have been fired
to signal the start of play.

C learly golf was a competitive game from the start. Though there was always pleasure in hitting a golf ball about in the company of one's friends – on a links, by the sea – the true delight was in acquiring the superior skill, becoming the better player. But how to prove it? The answer was 'matchplay', in which each hole was played and the player who hit the ball least often to hole out won the hole. No matter how many strokes were taken or by how many fewer than his opponent the winner scored, the result was one hole for the winner.

Any number of holes could be played in a match so long as the number was agreed at the start. If towards the end of a match one player was, say, 'three up' – three holes to the good – and there were only two holes to play then he was the winner, for even if his opponent won the remaining holes he would be one down.

This was the beginning of competitive golf. A match could be played by two people or four. In the latter case each two formed a team and hit the ball alternately – they played with one ball – against the other two, a form of golf known as a 'foursome'. Many years later there crept into golf the 'fourball' game, in which two players formed a team but each of the four players played his own ball and the score for the team was the lowest score by either player. To emphasize the distinction the foursome was sometimes called the 'two-ball foursome'.

Matches for major championships today are usually scheduled for 36 holes; a morning round is played and then, after a lunch break, comes an afternoon round. In practice, of course, such matches rarely last the 36 holes, though some close-fought ones can go into extra holes.

The single and the foursome were always regarded by the Royal and Ancient Golf Club of St Andrews as the true forms of golf, and even today it has few regulations concerning the fourball, preferring to ignore it. But the fourball game has become popular, and in North America the term foursome means a fourball. If Americans or Canadians want to make the distinction they talk of the two-ball foursome as a 'Scotch foursome'.

The early competitions were therefore single or foursome matches. The competitors were local friends and, one imagines, they played for no stake, or perhaps a very small one. But when the Stuart kings and their courts took up the game in the seventeenth century it became very fashionable, and heavy

(next page) An aerial view of the St Andrews course shows the links nature of the terrain.

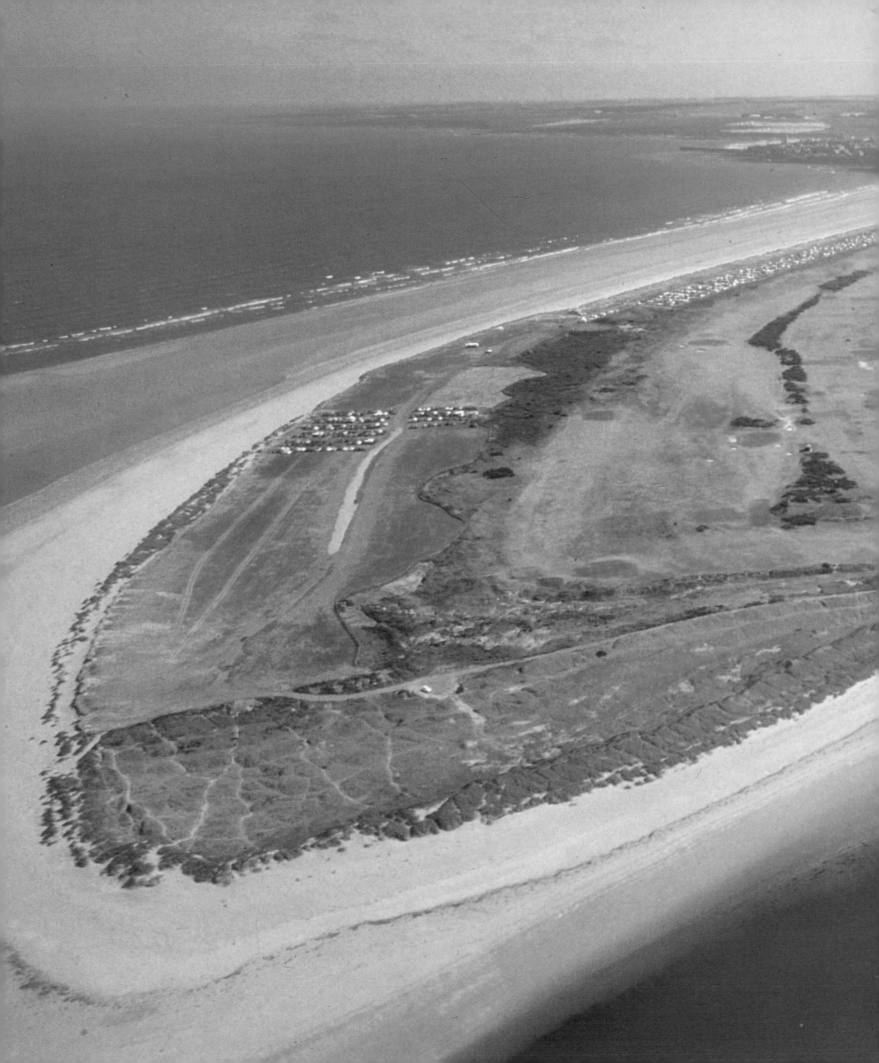

bets were placed on the outcome of matches. These were usually foursomes, frequently between two noblemen, each playing with a good golfer from a humbler walk of life. Occasionally a nobleman would play with a professional, but this was not common until the eighteenth century. Tales of some of the big-money challenge matches have taken their place in golfing lore; two are given here.

In 1682 the Duke of York – later James II – was challenged by two Englishmen – members of his entourage – to partner a fellow Scot against them for a big stake. He accepted and chose John Patersone, a poor Edinburgh shoemaker. Patersone was a very good golfer and the two Scots won easily. The amount of the stake is not known, but it was big enough for Patersone to buy a house in Edinburgh's fashionable Canongate with his share of it.

Nearly 200 years later another historic match was played, this time at the St Andrews Old Course, a contest immortalized by the painter Charles Lees, of the Royal Scottish Academy, in *The Grand Golf Match, 1850*. The picture communicates the tension and excitement as the players – four landed gentry – caddies and spectators wait to see if the critical putt will 'drop'. Many prints were later made from the painting, which typifies the competitive golfing scene in the late eighteenth and early nineteenth centuries.

At that time there were no tournament professionals as we know them, men making their living solely out of their proficiency at golf. The 'professional' of the day lived by making golf clubs and balls, giving a very occasional lesson and, when things were slack, caddying. In the winter, when no golf was played, he was unemployed unless he had a second line of work.

Though matchplay was the predominant form of golf competition, stroke play, also known as score play – or 'medal play', for it was usually played for a medal – was already a part of competition golf. In this game every stroke is counted, from the drive off the first tee to the last putt into the hole on the final green. The winner was the player who completed the course with the smallest number of strokes. It was customary to note down the score at each hole on a card and add up all the strokes at the end of the round. The first stroke play tournament took place at St Andrews about 1759. An entry in the minute book of the Royal and Ancient, dated May of that year, notes the beginning of stroke play:

> In order to remove all disputes and inconveniences with regard to the gaining of the Silver Club [first competed for there in 1754] it is enacted and agreed by the captain and the gentleman golfers present, that in all time coming whoever puts in the ball at the fewest strokes over the field, being 22 holes [the St Andrews course at the time], shall be declared and sustained victor.

At Blackheath the Silver Club was first played for in 1766, the Spring Gold Medal in 1797. The Gold Medal of the Honourable Company of Edinburgh Golfers was first competed for in 1790 and their Silver Club in 1744. This was the first formal competition golf of any kind and was a match in which the winner was the player who took most holes. First contention for the Royal and Ancient Gold Medal was in 1806. Such medal play was well known but not too popular, and on several occasions over the years there were no entries for the Silver Club.

An early caddie. No shoes,
no golf bag.

next page:
(left) The historic Open
Championship Cup, made in 1873,
is in fact a claret jug, a reminder of
the lavish wining and dining that
went on in the early days of the
Golf Clubs.

(right) The Open Championship
Belt, of handsome red morocco
leather bearing golfing scenes in
silver, was presented by Prestwick
Golf Club. Prestwick inaugurated
the Open, and it was later taken
over by the Royal and Ancient Golf
Club of St Andrews.

Real tournament golf, open to all and with the aim of identifying a champion, started in 1860, when eight professionals competed over three rounds of
12 holes each at Prestwick. They played for a red morocco leather Challenge
Belt that would become the permanent possession of whomever could win
the tournament three years running. The Belt attracted only a small entry at
the start but went on from strength to strength. The idea of competing for a
belt is said to have derived from mediaeval Knights' Tournaments, in which it
symbolized the champion. This was also doubtless the origin of the boxing
world's Lonsdale Belt, which also became the property of the gladiator who
won it for three consecutive years.

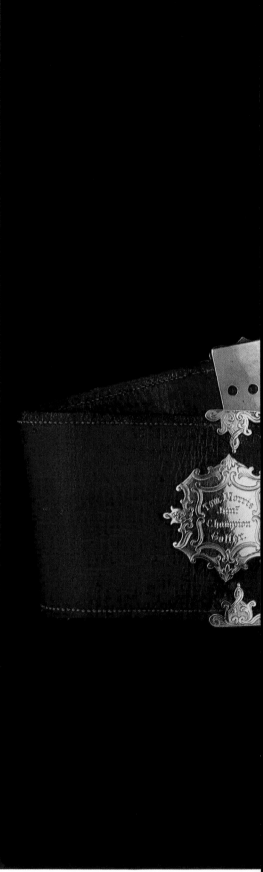

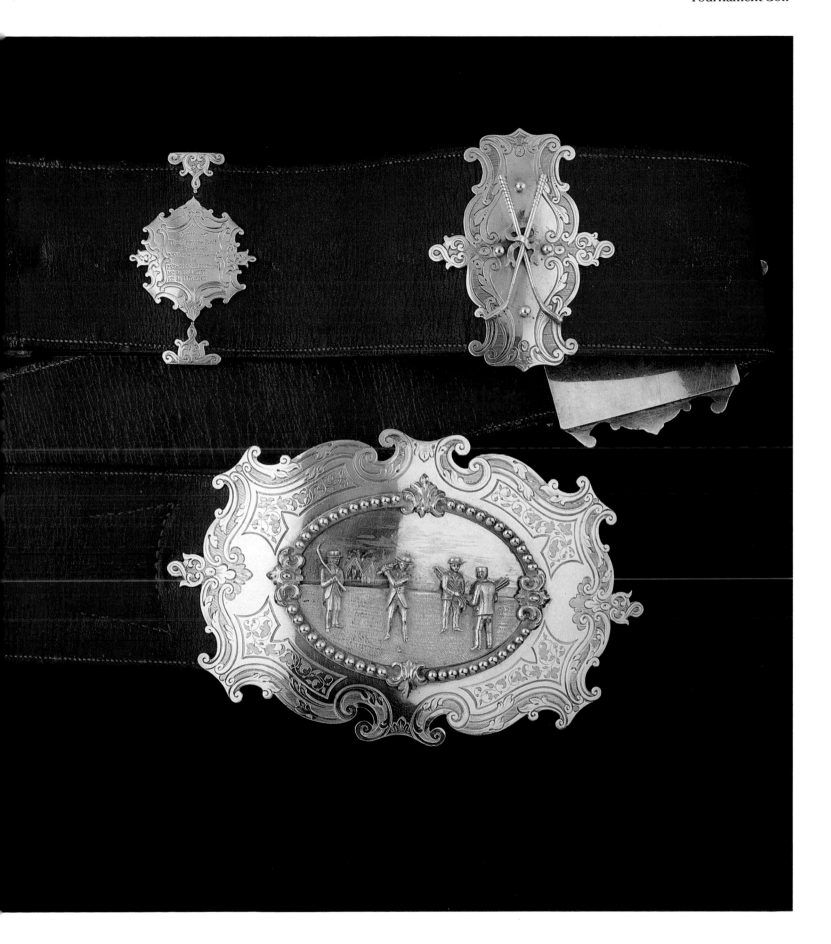

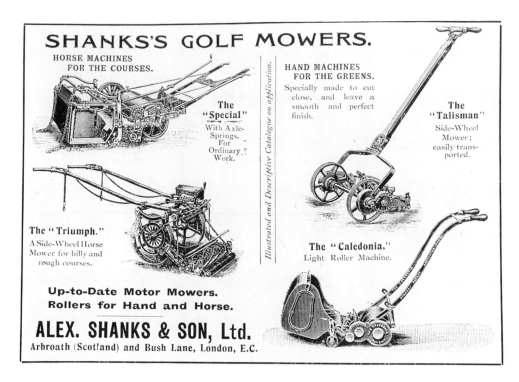

The first grass mowers revolutionized golf. Once grass could be cut quickly and at will a golf course could be laid almost anywhere.

This first championship was not, strictly speaking, the first Open Championship for it was restricted to professionals. But in the following year it became truly 'open to the world' and has been so ever since. Even now, in these days of prestigious golfing events like the US Open, the Open Championship – Americans call it the British Open – is regarded by many as the championship of the world.

The 1860 Championship, a medal competition, was won by Willie Park with a score of 174 for the 36 holes. The entry of eight might seem pretty small, but it must be remembered that there were very few professionals at that time. The golfing world was a small one, with only 38 Golf Clubs in existence – 34 in Scotland, one in England, one in Calcutta and two in the United States – and not every Club had a professional.

Park got no prize money for winning the first Open. The red leather and silver Championship Belt was considered to be enough. But three years later there was added a £5 money prize, and the Championship continued on these lines until the period 1868-70, when 'Young Tom' Morris won the Belt three times in a row and so kept it. There was a gap in 1871, for no one came forward to offer a substitute for the Belt, but in 1872 a Championship Cup was presented jointly by Prestwick, St Andrews and Musselburgh on the condition that the Championship be played over 36 holes in rotation at those Clubs. The Cup was to be a perpetual Challenge Cup and could not be won outright.

In 1880 there was a £20 money prize and a 'gold' medal for the winner, while those in second and third place got smaller amounts and a silver and bronze medal respectively. Thus winning the 'Open' in those days did not mean a pot of gold for the winner. Indeed Jamie Anderson, who won it three times in succession – 1877, 1878 and 1879 – died in the Poor House at Dysart, near Perth. Bob Ferguson, who also won the Championship three times in a row, spent the latter part of his life as a caddie at Musselburgh – the scene of one of his triumphs – and was unemployed in winter. Bob Martin, twice winner of the Open, returned to work on the railway.

The British Open Amateur Golf Trophy, a large and handsome silver cup decorated with golfing scenes, was first presented in 1886.

next page:
(left) Hazards, natural and artificial, give golf much of its zest. The devious mind of Heath Robinson produced its own zany obstacle course.

(right) A becapped Cupid caddies for a glamorous lady golfer in *La Vie Parisienne*'s rarified version of the game.

60e Année. N° 38   Le Numéro : I fr. 50   Samedi 23 Septembre 1922

LA VIE PARISIENNE

Herouard

Rédaction, Administration et Publicité : 29, rue Tronchet, Paris.

Nor was the Open Gold Medal itself of much intrinsic worth, being partly of silver gilt and partly of base metal. When in later years Willie Park Junior won the Open he sent the medal back to the Royal and Ancient, saying that if the cheap medal was the best they could do they had better keep it.

Apart from competing in a few local Scottish tournaments the only way to make a living at golf was by playing challenge matches. The pattern of these had changed and few amateurs were now involved, for the pros were now the better players and so attracted the backers' money. Generally two professionals would play each other, or four pros would play a two-ball foursome. As well as the prize money put up by backers there would be heavy betting. By these means, and by being Club professionals on small retainers – giving lessons and making clubs – a small number of pro golfers managed to make a living. But even they had a thin time in winter.

Some players were more involved in challenge matches than others. Always ready to back their skills against others' were such as Jamie and Willie Dunn of North Berwick and Blackheath; various members of the Morris family; Allan Robertson of St Andrews (a superb golfer who died the year before the first Open); John Allan of Westward Ho!; Robert Kirk of Hoylake; the Parks, father and son, of Musselburgh; and wee Ben Sayers, one-time acrobat, of North Berwick. But, except for the Parks, all of them kept secure jobs at Clubs, made clubs and gave lessons to local members, assuring themselves of a steady income.

The Parks, Senior and Junior, were attached to no Golf Club but made clubs on their own premises at Musselburgh. They played many challenge matches, and Willie Park Senior, the first Open Champion, ran an advertisement continuously for nine years in *Bell's Life* (later *Sporting Life*) offering to play any man in the world a 'home and home' match for £100. This was a match in which one round was played on the home links of one professional and a second on that of the other. Park particularly challenged Allan Robertson, but Robertson never took the bait; £100 was a lot of money in those days.

Willie Park Junior followed in his father's footsteps, but by 1889 had become so busy with his clubmaking shop at Musselburgh and his business as a golf course architect – he laid out courses not only in Britain but also in France, Canada and the US – that he had no more time for challenge matches. Anyway, he was now out of practice. It could be said that the Parks, unattached to any Club and making a freelance living from their golfing skills, were the earliest tournament professionals.

In 1892 the Open was played for the first time over four rounds of 18 holes. That year the prize money was £100, there were 30 entrants and, also for the first time, an entrance fee was charged. Amateur Harold Hilton won it, proving that it was really 'open'.

From 1894 until 1914 the Open was dominated by the Great Triumvirate – Harry Vardon, John Henry Taylor and James Braid. Taylor came first. He not only won at Sandwich in '94 – the number of courses for the Open had been extended – but the following year won again at St Andrews, becoming the first English winner in Scotland. All three golfers were associated with Clubs, but they spent most of their time giving exhibitions and playing in tournaments. By the turn of the century the numbers of both exhibition matches and tournaments had increased considerably and had supplanted the old challenge matches.

The Triumvirate's domination of of the Open was broken twice. In 1902 it

Harry Vardon follows through superbly on a tee shot despite a buttoned-up jacket. The other player is Ted Ray. The metal box marked '6' contains sand for making tees.

was won by Alexander ('Sandy') Herd, at Hoylake, near Liverpool, using the new American golf ball of wound rubber, but the Triumvirate soon learned to play with the new ball and resumed their domination. Then in 1907, Arnaud Massy, a Frenchman, won the event. For the first time the Continent showed itself capable of winning a major contest against the assembled Scottish and English might.

Meanwhile tournament golf had been developing in the United States. As we have seen, golf had been successfully established at Savannah and Charleston at the end of the eighteenth century, introduced by American Freemasons of Scottish descent whose families had come from Leith. But the Civil War and the unrest preceding it eclipsed these activities and golf did not reappear until 1888 at Yonkers, where the St Andrews Club was formed by the Apple Tree Gang.

In 1891 the first real American golf course, together with an architect-designed, purpose-built Clubhouse, was laid out at Shinnecock Hills, Long Island. Willie Dunn, of North Berwick, designed the course and US architect Stanford White the clubhouse. The United States Golf Association held its Open and Amateur Championships there in 1896, and in 1986 returned there for the Open as a gesture to the game's historic traditions.

As the Americans had been sending hickory golf club shafts to Britain since 1830 it may be wondered why, considering the early beginnings at Savannah and Charleston, there had been such a long lull before this initiative. The explanation may be that even when the Civil War was over there was much devastation and poverty in the South, the great estates were broken up and

A silver sculpture of Harry Vardon
from an original 1899 bronze by
Hal Ludlow.

A bronze statuette of legendary
ladies' golf champion Joyce
Wethered, now Lady Heathcoat
Amory. She won the British Ladies'
Open in 1922-24-25-29 and the
English Ladies' Close
Championship five years running
from 1920 to 1924.

Male golfing *chic* according to *Harper's*, 1898. The knickerbockers are sensible, but the jacket would hamper a chap's swing.

Tom Morris: Father and Son

'Old Tom' Morris, was a natural Keeper of the Green, born, raised and trained at St Andrews, where he was apprenticed to the famous golfer and feather ball- and clubmaker, Allan Robertson. In 1848 the two fell out when Morris broke a promise never to use the new-fangled gutta-percha balls that threatened Robertson's trade, and Tom moved to Prestwick.

Old Tom won the Open Championship Belt four times and played many historic challenge matches. In one such he and Allan Robertson took on the formidable twins, Willie and Jamie Dunn of Musselburgh, for the then huge stake of £400, the match to be played at Musselburgh, St Andrews and North Berwick. It was a time of great rivalry between St Andrews and Musselburgh, and there were big crowds, betting heavily. The Dunns won at Musselburgh but Tom and Robertson won at St Andrews, then took the North Berwick decider – largely, it is said, through Tom's calm resolution.

If Old Tom was great, Young Tom was the unbeatable genius of his day, playing shots that no one else would attempt. In his brief career – he died aged 25 – he played many challenge matches and won them all. At 17 he won his first Open Championship, over 27 holes, with a record score of 154, won again the next year with 157 and the year after with 149. The three consecutive wins made the Belt his own. Thereafter the Open was played for a 'perpetual' Cup.

1. 'Old' Tom in the 1860s.

2. Tom Sen. tees up the ball for the Royal and Ancient's new Captain. Behind him is the starter's box. A cannon was fired to herald the shot.

3. *(far left)* Grizzled and weathered, an older Old Tom

4, 5. Front and back view of the Open Championship Medal, of gold plate on base metal, which was provided annually after Young Tom won the Belt outright in 1870.

1872
WON BY
Thomas Morris Jr
PRESTWICK
166 STROKES

6. Tom Jun. wearing the Open Championship Belt. It became his when he won it three years running.

109

there was no more slave labour. Golf had been a pastime of the days of leisure and plenty. Now the South was putting its house in order and was too busy for games. Furthermore the Northern states may have been in no hurry to take up a game that they perceived to be Southern in origin.

But once golf did get started again, in 1888, it developed and spread at an incredible pace. By the turn of the century there were 26 Clubs in the Chicago area alone, urged on by Charles Blair MacDonald, a ferociously determined man who as a student had taken up golf at St Andrews. MacDonald designed the Chicago Golf Club, an excellent course, and later built the National Golf Links, not far from Shinnecock Hills. He managed to insinuate himself into anything that was going on in connection with the attractive new game.

In the West, to a somewhat lesser extent, Golf Clubs sprang up like mushrooms, for there was no shortage of players, though they were mainly people with money and leisure. They were not very expert as yet but were keen to learn, and to be sure of the finest instruction they imported professionals from Scotland, England and Canada. Golf was already widely played in Canada at this time. The first Club had been established at Montreal in 1873, while Quebec Golf Club was founded in the following year and the Toronto Club in 1876.

The US Golf Association was founded in 1894 and the first United States Amateur Championship was under way, 20 entrants playing 36 holes of medal play. The first five Championships were won by golfers who had learned their game in Britain, but in 1899 the first 'all-American' champion, Herbert Harriman, emerged. The United States Open Championship also started in 1894 but was not won by a home-bred player until 1911, when Johnny McDermott won and it began to be taken more seriously. Until then it had been regarded as less important than the US Amateur. After McDermott's victory US golfers took heart and began to dominate their own championship.

These American golfers, taught by mainly British professionals, were coming on fast. They were keen to develop, regarding golf as an important sport, and because of this they made a move which was to prove of tremendous value to the American game: they supported the development of college golf. Today intercollegiate golf is a major US enterprise. Colleges compete in first-class schedules and draw applicants for golf scholarships from all over the world.

In 1904 came an important event for American golfing morale. A US player called Walter J. Travis, unknown in Britain, crossed the Atlantic and won the British Amateur Championship. This was quite an achievement considering that at that time no American golfers had yet won their own Open, nor, until only two years before, their own Amateur. This somewhat crotchety American won using a new-fangled centre-shafted putter, the Schenectady, borrowed from a friend only the day before, and it was on the green that he proved so superior to the British players. The Royal and Ancient later banned centre-shafted putters, thereby adding martyrdom to prowess, and Travis became a folk hero back home. The British, it was said, had petulantly banned his putter because he was so good and they wanted to prevent his winning again. The Royal and Ancient vigorously denied such a motive. Centre-shafted putters were eventually approved.

Travis's triumph – though Australian-born he had been brought up in America from age six – encouraged other American amateurs to feel that they

(previous page) The beautiful scenery of California's Cypress Point may compensate a little for the brutal bunkers surrounding the 15th hole.

The 18th hole at St Andrews during a major tournament. A well-behaved crowd is marshalled by white-coated stewards and some local police.

Crowds run to see the next shot in a 1920s tournament at Cooden Beach, an excited cleric outrunning the young ladies. Note the several shooting sticks in evidence.

could now take on the British and beat them, a view that was somewhat premature. Only four years earlier they had had a real eye-opener when the great Harry Vardon had made his first American tour. Americans saw for the first time one of the truly great golfers in action, playing with a grace, power, and accuracy that they had scarcely imagined possible. The American re-action to Vardon was predictable: they must watch him and discover how it was done. Vardon recalls that after every shot spectators would ask one another with which hand he appeared to have hit the ball. He spent nine months in America, playing many matches and giving countless exhibitions, and wherever he played crowds turned out to see him. He was beaten only twice during the tour, a remarkable achievement considering that he was travelling vast distances by train to play on courses he had never seen before. Wherever he played or gave an exhibition the shops and businesses in the area would close for the day, and on one occasion, when he played near New York, the Stock Exchange closed for the afternoon! One result of his tour was a large increase in the number of American golfers and a corresponding growth in sales of clubs and balls.

During the nine months of Vardon's tour the 1901 US Open Championship was played, a memorable contest for the American public because not only was Vardon an entrant but so too was that other British 'great', J. H. Taylor. The result was fairly predictable: Harry Vardon won (by nine shots), Taylor was second and the third man was eight shots behind Taylor. That US Open drew a record crowd.

If the Americans were impressed by Vardon, he was impressed by their keenness to learn and improve. He forecast an eventual invasion by US golfers of the British scene and believed they would be a force to reckon with. Time has proved just how right he was! A year later, when Travis took Britain – and the British Amateur – by surprise, Vardon himself said he was not at all surprised.

In 1911 Americans got a further display of the standards set by top British amateurs when Harold Hilton crossed the Atlantic and won the US Amateur Championship. He remains the only British winner. This win may finally have put Americans on their mettle, making them even more determined to achieve the highest standards of play, to learn 'how it's done'. Through a scientific and studied approach to the game and an indefatigable willingness

Three Great Golfers: The Triumvirate

Three professionals dominated the British golfing scene during the 21 years from 1894 to 1914 and they came to be known as The Great Triumvirate. Between them they won, besides many other tournaments, the Open Championship 16 times and were runners-up in it 12 times.

John Henry Taylor was born in 1871 at Northam, Devon, a mile from the Westward Ho! Golf Club where he later became a boy caddie. He won the Open five times. A short, thickset man, he played his best in a strong wind using a rather flat-footed swing that kept his feet firmly on the ground. In particular he mastered the art of the pitch shot to the green, claiming it to be superior to the older running approach shot.

James Braid, born at Earlsferry, Fife, Scotland, in 1870, was apprenticed as a carpenter but played golf whenever he could. He won the Open Championship five times in nine years. A tall, slim, quiet man, he was a noted long hitter, his swing being characterized by a beautiful hand action.

Harry Vardon was born at Grouville, Jersey, in 1870 and learned his golf as a caddie on the island. He won six Open Championships and had many other wins, including the US Open in 1900. He suffered chronic ill health, with long spells in sanatoria, but his golfing genius triumphed over adversity. His swing was the epitome of grace and timing and he hit the ball great distances with apparently little effort.

1. Braid drives off, demonstrating his balanced swing and notable hand action.

2. The Vardon Grip. The overlap suited Vardon's big hands.

3. (far right) Taylor displays his flat-footed swing.

4. *The Great Triumvirate*, painted by Clement Flower in 1913. From left to right, J. H. Taylor, James Braid, and Harry Vardon.

115

A historic occasion. The three men in the play-off for the 1913 US Open at Brookline, Mass., are Harry Vardon (left), 18-year-old local lad Francis Ouimet (centre) and Ted Ray (right). Ouimet won.

(below) Photographers at St Andrews, positioned to cover the first tee (left background in front of the Clubhouse) as well as the 18th green (right background in front of the stand).

to practise they were eventually to turn the tide in their favour.

Two years later Lord Northcliffe, proprietor of the London *Times*, sponsored Harry Vardon for a second American tour, this time accompanied by Edward ('Ted') Ray. Ray was a big man, of great physical strength, a flamboyant golfer who sported a large moustache and smoked his pipe while playing. He also played in a trilby hat, which usually fell off during his follow-through. If grace was Vardon's hallmark, power was Ray's. He had won the British Open in 1912, beating Braid, Vardon and Taylor.

The tour was a huge success. Crowds even bigger than those on Vardon's previous tour followed them everywhere. They won nearly all of their matches.

Midway during this triumphal progress the two went to play in the US Open Championship at the Country Club, at Brookline, Mass. The general feeling was that though a few top American professionals might give them a run for their money one of the Britishers was certain to win. But this proved to be right only as far as the US professionals were concerned. No one had taken account of a 20-year-old amateur called Francis Ouimet, a young man from Massachusetts, who tied with both Ray and Vardon for first place, then beat them both in the play-off next day! In the same Championship a young professional called Walter Hagen did well. Robert Tyre (Bobby) Jones was too young to compete but was among the spectators.

The effect of Ouimet's victory on the US golfing scene was electric. A folk hero of the 'local-boy-makes-good' variety was born. And as Ouimet was a product of high school golf, and a force in developing high school competition in his state, that branch of the game got a special morale-boost. Ouimet had grown up across the street from the Country Club and later had caddied there, seeing many top players in action. He was instrumental in organizing golf at Brookline High School and at 16 he won the Greater Boston Interscholastic Championship. Four years later he was the US Open champion.

The growth of golf in the US had been remarkable – from about 10 players

Elegantly dressed Walter Hagen driving in the 1924 Open at Hoylake, which he won by one shot, beating an Englishman, E. R. Whitcombe. It's clear that playing in a pullover is a fairly new idea.

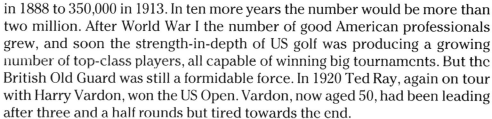

in 1888 to 350,000 in 1913. In ten more years the number would be more than two million. After World War I the number of good American professionals grew, and soon the strength-in-depth of US golf was producing a growing number of top-class players, all capable of winning big tournaments. But the British Old Guard was still a formidable force. In 1920 Ted Ray, again on tour with Harry Vardon, won the US Open. Vardon, now aged 50, had been leading after three and a half rounds but tired towards the end.

The Americans were soon to begin taking their revenge. In 1921 Jock Hutchison, American by adoption but born in St Andrews, where he had learnt his golf, won the British Open on his former home course. To soften their defeat the British could perhaps claim that though Hutchison was a US professional he had learned to play in Britain, but the next year the Open was taken by an indubitable American, Walter Hagen. US domination of world golf was on the way.

Hagen deserves special mention, not only because he was the first all-American winner of the British Open but also because he was the first of a new breed of professional golfers who recognized the need for showmanship in tournament golf and delivered it. He demanded – and got – financial rewards beyond the dreams of his predecessors, British or American.

The class system in British sport that regarded the amateur as the only genuine article, was to hold British professionals back for a further ten years, but the Americans had no such inhibitions. They were quick to build up the money side of the business as well as the 'showbiz' aspects of tournament golf, aspects which have developed steadily now for more than 50 years.

US professionals were fortunate in the sheer size of their country. When there was snow in the North the South was warm; when the South became too hot the North was just right for golf. The lengthening list of tournaments followed the sun and there was action all year round. Once born, the US tournament circuit grew by leaps and bounds. Financial rewards for the few at the top became enormous and there was no shortage of recruits to professional golf. Some, like Hagen, rose from the humble ranks of the caddies;

Sports d'Été et d'Hiver
Station d'altitude 1550 m. (5000 Feet)

MONTANA-VERMALA
S/SIERRE (SUISSE)

CHEMIN DE FER DU NORD
LE TOUQUET
Paris-Plage

GOLF: 45 Trous _ **TENNIS**: 30 Courts
CHAMP DE **COURSES** _ **PLAGE** DE SABLE
LA PLUS BELLE **PISCINE** D'EUROPE
66ᵐ66 de long sur 25ᵐ de large
Eau de mer réchauffée
CASINO DE LA **PLAGE** _ **CASINO** DE LA **FORÊT**

PRINTED IN FRANCE   LUCIEN SERRE & Cᵉ IMP. 15-17-19 Rue du Terrage, PARIS

others came from the great reservoir of inter-collegiate golfers. Whatever their origins, those who got to the top still had to work to stay there, being under constant pressure from an army of hard-working, constantly-practising, intense young golfers, all going for the big prize – as the stars themselves had gone for it.

Things were slower in Britain, partly because the British season has only six months of good golf weather. Top players could make a living at tournament golf but many of the less talented found life difficult. Some emigrated to the US, where they made a satisfactory living by teaching and working as Club professionals. There was less money in British professional golf and far fewer events. Only the Open carried enough prestige to make a visit worthwhile for an American, and tournament-hardened US professionals now took the Open Championship trophy off to America fairly regularly. Between 1920 and 1934 the British Open was won 11 times by American players, three times by boy wonder Bobby Jones.

Between the Wars golf had been developing also in other parts of the world, particularly in the Commonwealth – then still 'the Empire'. As we have seen, many British emigrants to those countries had taken with them their love for the game and their skills at it. After World War II some top-class Commonwealth professionals began to appear in the UK and soon made their presence felt.

Bobby Locke, from South Africa, won the British Open in 1949, 1950, 1952 and 1957. Australian Peter Thomson took it in 1954, 1955, 1956, 1958 and 1965. The American entry at this time was small, for it was more lucrative to be fifth in a US tournament than to win the British Open. It should be pointed out, too, that the British Open, though prestigious, lost some lustre as the US circuit developed.

The Commonwealth countries' own Open Championships had now assumed some importance, particularly the Canadian and Australian Opens,

(above) The face is not easily recognized but the beautifully balanced swing of young Bobby Jones is unmistakable. Note the boots, probably hobnailed for a good grip.

(left) Bobby does it again! Bobby Jones with the 1927 Open Trophy at St Andrews after the second of his three wins. In 1930 he won the US Open, US Amateur, British Open and British Amateur, an amateur record still unchallenged.

(previous page) Two posters of about 1930 advertising golf in Switzerland and France. Golf posters are becoming increasingly sought after for their graphic invention and colourful representation of the game.

Driving ranges abound in Japan, where the shortage of golf courses means that many golfers will never play on one.

(below) Gary Player jumps to see the bottom of the pin. Small but super-fit Player was the first foreigner to win the US Masters and first foreign winner of the US Open (1965) since Ted Ray's 1920 victory. He has won the US Open and the Masters three times each.

first established in 1904. These tournaments were both prestigious and remunerative, and international professionals found it worth their while to compete in them. The golf tournament circuit was expanding to include the whole world as improved air travel made it ever cheaper, easier and quicker to go to tournaments thousands of miles away. Shorter trips were also easier to make, and British professionals, long deprived of their game during winter – barring expensive American visits – now followed the sun to Southern Europe, then to Africa.

No professional from outside the USA has ever dominated the American golf circuit, though there have been many notable wins by such players as Gary Player, Severiano Ballesteros, Bernhard Langer, Isao Aoki and Greg Norman. Englishman Tony Jacklin did win the 1970 US Open but it was a one-off victory. Similarly, while US professionals have had their victories abroad they no longer have ascendancy on the foreign tournament scene. Other countries, notably Spain and Japan, are proving themselves in world tournament golf. While prize money continues to grow, satellite television brings virtually world-wide coverage of the major tournaments, increasing the possibilities of advertising and the non-tour earnings of the professional. Sponsoring – by club, ball and clothing manufacturers – 'appearance money', golf clinics during tournaments and so on have all combined to make the successful professional a big earner. A recent winner of the British Open Championship, Sandy Lyle, signed a contract with a whisky manufacturer that guarantees him £300,000 ($450,000) per year for three years plus a bonus for every tournament he wins – this on the strength of a single world championship! His other earnings from sponsorship are not disclosed.

Professional golf is no longer simply a sport but a very highly paid branch of the entertainment business. It is also an advertising medium for a multi-million-dollar industry that gives employment to thousands throughout the world.

View of the 10th green at Augusta, Georgia, on the final day of the 1984 Masters Tournament. This is widely recognized as one of the most beautiful golf courses in the world.

The Modern Game

James Barclay, *The Golfers*, etching, c.1920.

One of the big differences between today's golf and that of only thirty years ago is the huge increase in the number of tournaments – professional, amateur, ladies' and juniors'. The world-wide trail of the prestige golf tournaments is a path paved with gold. Top players will receive 'appearance money' – a fee for simply turning up at the tournament – and there is still more money to be made from films, from exhibition matches, from advertising, and from writing. For golfing megastars such as Jack Nicklaus, Severiano Ballesteros and Greg Norman the possibilities are endless – but the physical and mental demands are tremendous too.

The tournament circuit is a continuous year-long, world-wide round of activity. Golf has no 'close season'. There are no gaps in the calendar. At any time of the year there are countries with suitable golfing climates. The major circuit is the American PGA Tour, offering most of the highest purses, superb courses, a coordinated schedule and major big-business sponsors. Then there is the PGA European Tour, which has made tremendous gains in recent years and whose stars include such players as Ballesteros and Bernhard Langer. Just as the USA has always been the golfing home for such as Jack Nicklaus, Lee Trevino and Tom Watson, Ballesteros has made Europe 'golf central' to him.

After these tours the most important are the Japanese, Australian, Far East and African. The Japan Tour has its own full schedule, separate from the Far East, and promises to produce some world stars. Notable is Tsuneyuki Nakajima, who has already done fairly well in the US, where he is known as Tommy.

Australia is a golfing power to be reckoned with, though that country's contribution to the world game is often overlooked, perhaps because its top performers inevitably spend so much time in the US. That Australia is a breeding ground for golfing talent is attested by the successes of players like Bruce Crampton, Bruce Devlin, David Graham, Peter Thomson and Greg Norman, the last being *the* Australian star.

The professional golf scene may be compared with the film industry. It has its 'extras', whose earnings are small and irregular. Then there are the 'bit players', not stars but competent professionals who make a good living by regular hard work. At the top are the stars and megastars – only about 200-300 of them worldwide – living in the glare of the limelight and earning

(left) Bernhard Langer, the first German golfing megastar and a highly popular player, has won championships worldwide, including the US Masters 1985, the European Open 1985 and the Australian Masters 1986.

(right) Many golf courses are designed to take advantage of the natural topography. Here the local rhododendrons are in full flower at the immaculate Augusta course during a US Masters.

'Eyes and ears of the world.' Professional golf is now a television spectacular for millions of armchair experts.

enormous sums. They are forever in the public eye, their private lives public knowledge. But stardom can be fleeting. In a fiercely competitive environment there is a constant siege from hungry new talent rising from the ranks below.

Golfers are uniquely addicted to their sport. The amateur knows the occasional feeling of swinging well for 18 holes or hitting a shot just right, and is convinced that he can repeat the success next time. The pro player has this feeling virtually permanently, and feels sure that he can one day win a big tournament. Furthermore, pro golfers' working lives are longer than those of other sportsmen and women, many of whom find their careers are already over at 35, so golfers feel that time is on their side. All this is what keeps the 'bit players' going. Work hard, they believe, and you will succeed – which is not necessarily true.

Continuing the movie analogy, there are also many others on the fringe – agents, managers, cameramen, ad-men, tournament organizers – who make a good living from the great golfing occasions. And because the major world tournaments attract enormous television viewing figures, an army of commentators and technicians follows the golden circuit, recording all the drama, beauty and excitement and providing a ringside seat for millions of armchair golfers. Golf is a natural television spectacle, almost invariably played in beautiful places – some, like Augusta National in the United States, so beautiful that they can upstage the competition itself! There is the beauty of the greens, the blue water and the trees; there are the colourful outfits of the players; and there is the atmosphere of excitement – greatly enhanced by huge eager crowds. Crowds are a TV director's delight, thousands of extras to heighten the tension. And because the golf course changes from tournament to tournament television has the unique challenge of presenting the problems of the game whatever the landscape.

But the television fraternity lead a nerve-racking life, for a golf tournament is very much live entertainment. There can be no retakes, and occasionally the spectacular is hit by sudden bad weather, leaving a yawning gap in broadcasting schedules. This is rare, but even if it does happen a bright television man can turn it to account. On one such occasion in the United States the camera team saved the situation by getting a group of top golfers to stand and chat with 100 or so spectators. The viewers loved it. They got to know aspects of the players that could never have emerged while they were concentrating on their game.

It is only in Britain that the Open Championship observes the tradition of true links golf. Links courses, with no trees and no landscaping or artificial lakes, present quite a different television picture. Courses like the Old Course at St Andrews, the Royal St George's, at Sandwich, and Muirfield, in Gullane, lack colour and are basically flat, though with a great many 'umps' and 'ollers' – rough, deep bunkers and a sand dune or two. In these links championships the players face a difficulty that is not easily communicated by television – winds, blowing hard across the open terrain, that can change their speed and direction in minutes, making distance markers almost worthless and ball control difficult.

There could not be a greater contrast than that between these rather bleak British links courses and the superbly landscaped 'stadium' courses now to be seen, notably in North America. Designed with the spectators in mind, they are usually sited among low hills that form natural amphitheatres. Augusta

'We've won the Ryder Cup!' Great Britain and Europe win the 1985 Ryder Cup and Ballesteros sprays non-playing captain Tony Jacklin with bubbly, to the amusement of Sam Torrance and Bernhard Langer.

A sharply bowed flag reveals the invisible hazard faced by golfers on windswept seaside links courses.

(next page) A beautiful Spanish course between mountains and sea at Aloha, one of the innumerable golf courses on the Costa del Sol.

National, mentioned above, was perhaps the first of these and another is Glen Abbey, near Toronto, Canada, designed by Jack Nicklaus and now the permanent site of the Canadian Open.

What the links courses lack in beauty they make up for in history, and television commentators can usually convey that history, as well as the special problems that players face on them.

To maintain form a top professional golfer must practise regularly for several hours daily, and for increasingly longer periods if he or she has a particular problem. The professional's putting stroke probably gets the closest attention, for this part of the game is vital for success. Victory in a tournament is almost invariably due to the ability to hole the putts. A short putt counts the same as a 290-yard drive, but whereas the drive is as near to a natural reflex action as any golf stroke can be, the putt involves intense concentration, determination and a delicate sense of touch. It is a make-or-break shot. Miss a tee shot or a second shot and there is usually a chance of a good recovery that may allow par. But you cannot recover after missing a

The Modern Professional: Jack Nicklaus

The American Jack William Nicklaus is a golfing mega-star who follows the tournament circuits in his own jet plane, flown by his own pilot. He has earned well over $5,000,000 in prize money alone.

Nicklaus, born in 1940, was a noted amateur. He went to Ohio State University on a golf scholarship, and in 1959 he became the youngest-ever US Amateur Champion. He also represented his country in that year's Walker Cup Match at Muirfield, Scotland, winning his singles and foursomes.

In 1961 he turned professional, and his victories since then read like a roll of golfing battle honours: The Open Championship – three times; the US Open – four times; the US Masters – six times; the US PGA – five times; the Australian Open – six times; and numerous other major tournament victories.

Nicklaus's business interests are legion. He promotes golf equipment in the USA and abroad, and he also endorses brands of shoes and clothes. He has written several books and numerous golfing articles and golf tips that are circulated in some 100 newspapers worldwide. He is also a noted golf architect and has designed many fine courses.

opposite:

3. Bernhard Langer, the previous winner, helps Nicklaus into the victor's green jacket at the 1986 US Masters.

4. Bunkered! Nicklaus keeping his (slightly worried) eye on the ball.

5. Sizing up a putt.

6. Tom Watson and Jack Nicklaus, Ryder Cup compatriots, study a putt.

7. *(centre)* Nicklaus shows off his latest prize – the British Open trophy (July 1978).

2. Jack's son has frequently caddied for his father.

1. The face of a champion: a blend of concentration, judgement and physical effort.

3

4

5

6

(right) Glen Abbey, Ontario, site of the Canadian Open, is considered by many to be a tough course to play. Designed by Jack Nicklaus, it is an excellent example of modern course architecture.

Massed umbrellas at the US Masters show that even in Georgia sunshine is not certain.

Ballesteros considers a putt like a Grand Master gravely plotting a chess move. The outcome of a tournament – and a big purse – often hangs on a single putt.

(below) Greg Norman in self-communion before a crucial putt. This is when the professional's iron nerve and self-confidence are tested.

short putt. The pro must master a putting stroke that can be relied on even when under pressure.

Few professionals will change any of their clubs without much consideration and a thorough trial. But putters are a different matter. A nice-feeling putter may be found anywhere, and it may be of any age. If it feels right a pro may take it out on the next round after only a brief trial. Putting is largely a matter of confidence, and the wise golfer welcomes anything that will create it, be it a new putter or a lucky talisman in the pocket. When Jack Nicklaus won the 1986 US Masters his victory was due to superb putting with an unattractive oversize club. Immediately some 50,000 Nicklaus putters were ordered by American golfers.

Increasingly golfers have coaches, and some, like Jack Nicklaus, will stick with one coach throughout a golfing career while others will go from teacher to teacher for help. Pros feel that the game is largely psychological, and recently there has appeared a cadre of sports psychologists. These teach players to control and use their emotions, to visualize the flight of the ball before swinging, to imagine themselves successfully dealing with situations in advance, to remember comfortable situations when they are ill at ease. Anything for success at the game: Ray Floyd admits to bizarre mental procedures to gain confidence before a difficult shot.

Rain halts play. Staff 'squeegee' standing water off a green so that the game may resume.

(below) Caddies have come along way since schoolboys carried clubs for a shilling. A top caddie today can make as much as $100,000 per year. Here the waistcoat tells all.

Not only the players prepare earnestly for a tournament. Caddies too are at work from the early hours of a tournament day, 'walking the course', noting tee positions and any particular difficulties of the layout. One never knows when some scrap of extra information will help a player to put the ball in the right place. Caddies also check the yardage between a given marker and the front edge of the green. They measure the distance between each pin and the front of the green so that players will know the exact distance of any shot. This procedure has recently become less important as tournament officials now hand out 'pin sheets' to players on the first tee. The sheets indicate pin placements for the day relative to the length and breadth of greens. By combining the information on the sheet with that learned during practice rounds a player can work out, say, the overall length of a shot from a particular marker.

The host Golf Club, sponsors and officials also undertake painstaking preparations before staging a major tournament. Most tournaments rely on a large cadre of volunteers to help run things. They work as scorers, hospitality agents, parking officials, crowd controllers and drivers for shuttling the players between their hotels and the course.

Months before the tournament the greens staff, perhaps with some outside help, start preparing the course with the aim of bringing it up to peak con-

dition. Certain decisions must be taken about where to grow the rough in, how to narrow the fairways at certain strategic points, which tees shall be used, whether special tees – to test the competitors or for easier crowd control – will be necessary. The better condition a course is in from day to day the easier it will be to bring it up to tournament level. A major tournament is sometimes called 'an examination in golf', aimed at identifying the current best player in the world, and it is to this end that the course is prepared with 'problems' that will reveal a player's touch – or lack of it.

Also required are electronic scoreboards, which at the biggest events must be placed at various points all over the course to receive continuous information from score recorders equipped with walkie-talkies. Instant information is vital, both to spectators and to the attendant media. The recorders will be stationed at each hole to ask players or their scorers, as they come off a green, what the score was at that hole.

With a major tournament in view there must be very careful consideration of the local rules and their interpretation. Competition is ferocious nowadays and little is left of the 'spirit of the game' attitude accepted by earlier generations of golfers. Rules clearly laid down will be obeyed, for pro golfers are great respecters of the rules, but any ambiguity will be aggressively seized upon and exploited. Golf is a game full of situations that are open to interpretation, and any player's legitimate interest is to try for a favourable ruling. As a result of all this there have now evolved 'tournament rules', which are different from the rules by which lesser mortals are expected to play.

Nevertheless a sort of sporting chivalry on the course is not unknown. Players have called penalties against themselves when a ball has moved, though no one else has noticed. Occasionally golfers have found an extra club in the bag and declared it, accepting the penalty.

Tournament rules must take into account the presence these days of spectator stands and television towers at major events. There is a 'line of sight' rule which allows a player a free drop if his view of the flag is obstructed by such impedimenta. Even though the obstruction is many yards from the player he may drop to one side to get a clear view of the flag. Then there is the 'free dropping zone'. Because stands and towers are fairly close to greens a wide shot can finish up beneath one or the other. If this happens the player is allowed a free drop in a specified 'dropping zone' that will give an unimpeded

(above) The commentators' box, with a very distinguished golfer and commentator, the late Henry Longhurst.

(top) Never mind the grammar – read the message! An electronic scoreboard celebrates the fringe pleasures of a golfing day out in the sun.

(right) A durable US pro is Don January, winner of the 1967 American PGA Championship but of few other major events. Yet he is so consistent, and so consistently 'placed', that by 1979 his winnings topped $1 million. He is now one of the most successful competitors in senior tournaments.

Branches everywhere. After hooking into the trees during the World Matchplay Championship at Wentworth (1986) Sandy Lyle urges the crowd to a safe distance before trying to get out.

swing and a clear view of the flag. Thus it is possible for a wild shot – which in normal circumstances would finish in a wood or thick grass, or even out of bounds – to be rewarded by a free drop in much better conditions.

Despite these carefully thought-out rules it is necessary to send out an experienced golfer or official to referee each match, and even this may not be the end of it. Players have been known to question a referee's decision and to demand – and get – another referee.

The thousands of spectators who attend each day of a major championship will often find a great tented village that offers everything by way of side-shows and refreshments. There are stands advertising golfing holidays, displays of golfing clothes, golf clubs and balls, golf shoes, golf carts, golfing umbrellas, magazines, books and videos, golfing antiques and novelties, time-share properties in the world's favourite golfing regions. In Britain banks are open for business in the village and there are plenty of other marketing opportunities for non-golfing enterprises.

In short, a highly efficient and well-organized army of experts is mobilized to ensure that competitors are able to display their skills and to provide entertainment and excitement for the many thousands of on-the-spot spectators. At the same time no effort is spared to ensure that millions more, sitting comfortably at home, experience all the colour, drama and beauty of the tournament.

Senior Tournaments

For many years there has been a growing number of senior tournaments, special competitions for professionals who have passed the age of 50, and now, in the United States, there is a Senior Professional Golfers' Association Tour that has burgeoned into a major tour with nearly $10,000,000 in prize money.

In the UK the Senior Open Professional Tournament, consisting of three rounds of medal play, started in 1957. In 1961 a World Senior Matchplay Open Championship was inaugurated but was discontinued after 17 years.

The US Senior PGA Tour, with its rich prizes, attracts professionals from all over the world, some of them still playing on the main professional circuit. One such, Don January, had by 1985 won more than $1,000,000 in senior tournament golf. Such is now the level of prize money that past Open champ-

(right) Gene Sarazen, famous US pro of the twenties and thirties. A good all-round golfer, he was specially noted for his skill with the sand wedge. He won the US Open twice, the British Open once, the Masters once and the US PGA three times.

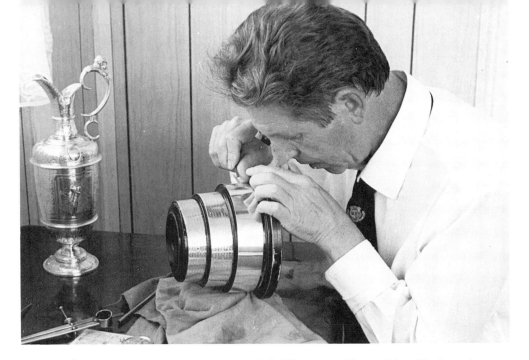

The Royal and Ancient's Alex Hervey engraves the Open Championship cup. He cannot start until the match is over and the winner known, but must have it finished for presentation time.

ions and other veteran pros, some with 20-year-old world golf victories to their credit, can now pick up more than ever they did in their heyday, when prizes were much smaller.

Senior golf is successful because golf is a game for all ages. Indeed there is now a Super-Senior section for golfers over 60, who can still produce some very good golf. They play in about 20 events presented concurrently with the main tournament, each offering a purse of $35,000 over 36 holes. On the Senior Tour pros and amateurs mix closely and there is a strong pro-am element, and each big event is preceded by a 36-hole pro-am game. Amateurs pay hefty sums for the privilege of partnering and competing against world class players.

One often hears the argument that those who play in the main tournaments *and* on the senior circuit should be allowed to play in only one. Such players as Bruce Crampton, C. C. Rodriguez and Gary Player compete in the senior tournaments. While the senior competition is tough most of these veterans, with records of success, are not fighting for a livelihood. They are already comfortably off and play mainly because they still like to compete and win.

There are now strong moves afoot to extend the senior circuit to Britain and the rest of Europe, and if this happens senior events will become bigger business, TV coverage will be extended, the money prizes will swell and a world-wide Senior Circuit may come into being.

Professional Golf Tournaments for Women

Women's professional golf, still a novelty 15 years ago, has made very rapid advances. At first it was confined to the United States, where the few women's professional events attracted little attention and the prizes were so meagre that a woman pro could scarcely make a living. Now the US women's circuit has become so attractive that every year young hopefuls have to go through a tough qualifying school, and the women's tour has also developed into big business in the UK, Europe and the Far East. In 1986 the US Ladies' Professional Golf Association played 36 events for $10,000,000. A respectable chunk of that huge sum was the $492,021 won by Pat Bradley.

In the last generation the quality of play has improved beyond recognition. True, some sponsors are still concerned with women's golfing fashions, but women's golf clubs are also big business. On the teaching side women golf

141

professionals are often better able to understand women golfers' problems, especially those associated with relative lack of physical strength, and so are better suited to instruct their own sex.

One effect of women's golf tournaments has been that of redressing the balance between putting and the long game. In men's golf the wooden club is employed almost entirely on the tee shot; it is very seldom needed for the second shot, except on long par fives, as an iron will suffice to reach the green. In women's golf, however, though drives of 240 yards are commonplace, players often have to play their second shots to the longer holes with fairway woods. Thus women's golf has re-introduced into the game the art of fairway wooden club play through the green, an art that has largely vanished from men's professional golf.

The Professional-Amateur Tournament

There has also been fast expansion in the sphere of Pro-Am Tournaments, in which teams of two or more players compete, each team comprising a professional playing with from one to three amateurs to produce a net best-ball team score between them, while the professionals also play for an individual prize. Only the lowest net score of the players in a team is recorded at each hole. Handicap strokes are given to the amateur players.

There are different types of Pro-Am competitions, the most prestigious being what was until recently called the *Bing Crosby*, at Pebble Beach, California, and the *Bob Hope Desert Classic*. The *'Crosby'* tournament consists of five rounds of medal play in which a professional partners one

(right) An elegant 1930s lady player tempts golfers to take their clubs abroad.

Jan Stephenson, Australian Women's Open Champion 1983 and British Ladies' Open Champion 1984, shows how to follow through – if you are supple enough.

golf de Sarlabot
houlgate – cabourg

Creating a Golf Course

Until 100 years ago all golf was played on natural terrain, usually sparse seaside turf cropped by sheep and rabbits, where the thin soil allowed good drainage. The bunkers were places where sheltering sheep had worn shallow topsoil down to the underlying sand. Greens were naturally flat patches.

But as the game spread inland – and to other countries – there arose a need for purpose-designed courses. A new breed of men, golf course architects, came into being, and over the years have proved themselves not only as landscaping artists but as specialist civil engineers. While drainage and contouring of heathland is fairly easy, in many parts of the world making a golf course entails clearing jungle, draining swamps and literally moving mountains.

Golf course designers face a unique challenge. They must provide enjoyment and a test of skill to players of very different abilities, and while they may wish a course to be a test of champions – and make it one – their cunningly sculpted terrain must also be playable by golfers of much more modest skills. Designers also have to ensure stimulating variety by contriving to make each of the 18 holes a different kind of challenge from all the others.

Shown here is a superb example of the art, the course at Lake Garda, Italy, designed by Donald Steel and opened in 1986.

1. To construct the greens contractors need detailed scale drawings of contour shapes, levels and bunkers.

2. Plan of the course at Lake Garda, near Salò.

Inset:

Before: The third fairway under construction, with surveying posts in place. Much ploughing reduced the heavy soil to a tilth fine enough for grass sowing.

After: The green at the short second hole. A stream was dammed to form the lake, and the back of the green was landscaped, incorporating the existing trees. The tee is much higher than the green, which was formed out of the hillside.

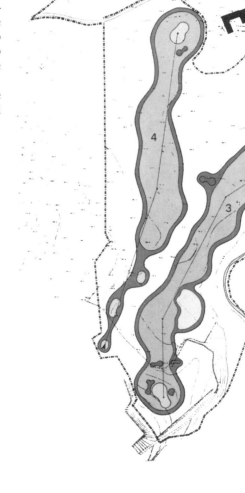

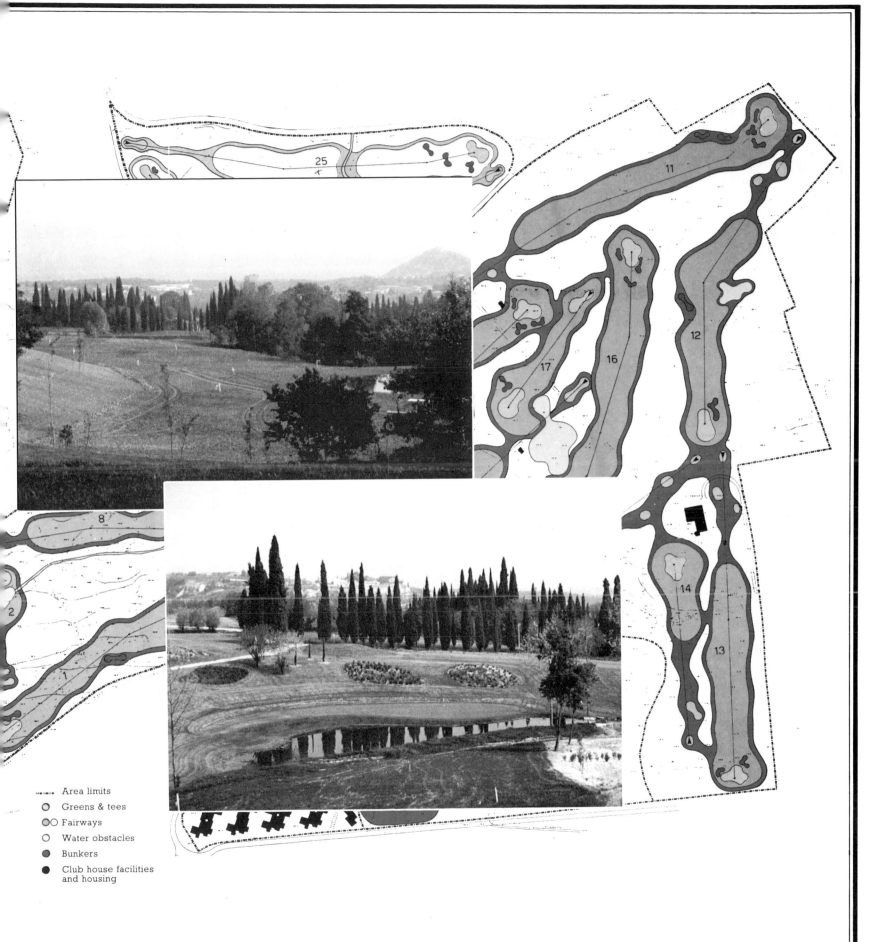

Area limits

Greens & tees

Fairways

Water obstacles

Bunkers

Club house facilities
and housing

amateur throughout. Though the *'Crosby'* demands a very high entrance fee there are always some 1,000 applications for its 200 places. Individual prizes for the professionals are juicy ones.

Another kind of Pro-Am is played on the day before a big tournament, when pros are keen to get in a practice round and the three amateurs who play with each pro may pay $1,000 or more for the privilege. In other Pro-Am tournaments teams consisting of a Club professional or assistant and two or three amateurs play a 36-hole medal game over two days. A tournament of this kind gives the Club pros a chance to play competitive golf, win a little prize money and enjoy a holiday in the sun – usually at the amateurs' expense. The amateurs have the thrill of playing tournament golf on a top course and the possibility of taking home a handsome trophy.

The Future

The future of professional golf seems assured. Only the best of the young hopefuls will survive, but that is the nature of the profession. Large numbers of people will always want to play the game, as they have for centuries. There will always be pleasure in directing a ball to its target with a perfectly designed implement. That appeal will surely not change.

What may change is the focus on individual national tours. A world tour could yet come about. Already the top players are international figures and already there is a world ranking system, the Sony Ranking. The major players of the world gather each year for the Nissan Cup, a team tournament, and though top pros earn a pittance by taking part in the Ryder Cup they are all keen. Representing their countries in the championship means more to them than a big cheque. There will always be a minor league of lesser players content to earn a living at the game, but the best – such as Ballesteros, Langer, Norman, Watson and Nicklaus – will go on playing the world in this most international of sports. It may be only a matter of time before we see a world super-tour for top players.

Such a tour would be fed through the individual tours – the American PGA, the European, the Japanese and the rest – and would require cooperation between the various administrations. It would also need a change in the present arrangements whereby American and European stars must obtain releases from their home tours to play elsewhere. Many top players feel they should be free to set their own schedules, and the forces favouring truly international golf would have to bring about such free movement.

Failing such cooperation some outside group might develop a world tour. The International Management Group, already involved in pro golf through tournaments and special events, springs to mind. IMG produce the Nissan Cup and the Suntory World Match Play Championship, held each year at Wentworth, near London. The Group is also behind the Sony Ranking system, which the Royal and Ancient uses to invite three players, otherwise ineligible, to the Open Championship.

The Fascination of Golf

Most of the huge amount of money spent on golf tournaments returns to the promoters with a handsome profit from the advertising media and increased product sales. Those who foot this mighty bill are the ordinary golfers, most of them not good players but dedicated to the game. They love to see it played

(previous page) Bernhard Langer driving in the British Open at Turnberry, a great links course set on a stretch of wild and beautiful coast.

It's no laughing matter, even for comedian Bob Hope, seen here being serious for once.

Gordon Brand (left) receives a giant cheque from Bob Hope after the Pro-Am, and actor James Garner looks on appreciatively.

Gordon Brand (left) receives a giant cheque from Bob Hope after the Pro-Am, and actor James Garner looks on appreciatively.

(next page) Pebble Beach, a magnificent golf course on the California coast, has been the venue of many major championships.

well, to read its stars on 'how it's done'. They buy clubs, balls and ancillary gear which, they hope, will improve their game. This astonishing enthusiasm – surely unparalleled in any other sport – has lasted 500 years and shows no sign of abating.

Of course golf has qualities that place it apart from other games. Not the least is that people of all ages can play it. You can start learning as soon as you can walk, and play it until you can walk no longer. While good players expect their shots to be good ones, the poor player goes out expecting the worst and can return with glowing memories of a few, perhaps lucky good shots – a happy state of affairs. At the same time the handicapping system, which fairly reflects players' abilities, allows indifferent golfers to enjoy a game with superior opponents or partners.

These factors alone would make golf a popular sport, but its history suggests something rather more – something, I suggest, in the nature of an obsession.

In Stuart times you could not play on wet days for fear of ruining the feather ball (cost: £20 in today's money). Rain could also damage wooden shafts, and on frosty days clubheads could split on the frozen ground. The links courses were rough, cluttered with debris and animal droppings. Yet golf was enthusiastically played – by the rich, who could afford costly new featheries, and by the poor, using old discarded ones, or even wooden balls, and damaged cast-off clubs. The love of golf, in such circumstances, went beyond mere enthusiasm.

An obsession, say the dictionaries, is something that takes possession of the mind – by inference exclusively – and there is no doubt that the word sums up many golfers' attitude to their game. There have been some acute cases.

Alexander McKellar and his wife were running an Edinburgh pub during the late eighteenth century when Alexander, late in life, discovered golf. He played on nearby Bruntsfield links and soon became obsessed with it. He was away with his clubs at first light every day except Sunday, leaving his wife to

carry on the business. He would play right through the day and even after dark, playing short holes by the light of a lanthorn. When his vexed wife tried to bring him to his senses by taking his nightcap and his dinner on a tray out to him on the darkened links he said he was too busy to stop. He often played alone, never joined Bruntsfield Club and, despite unremitting practice, remained a poor player. Alexander's keenness earned him cachet as a local character and the nickname 'Cock o' the Green'.

Another golf-obsessed Scot was a tea planter in Assam early this century. The only white man on the estate, his nearest neighbours were 50 jungle miles away, but he was determined to play golf. He had no golf course and no one to play with so he had his labour force hack a three-hole course out of the jungle, meanwhile teaching his houseboy to use a club. The night before the great day when they were going to play their first game an earthquake wiped out two of the holes. The men were set to work replacing them, and after some weeks the course was again ready. They were to play in the morning, but the poor planter died of a heart attack. His faithful servants buried him behind the third green.

Such examples – and there are thousands of others – testify to the obsessive potential of golf. But what gives it that special quality? One answer may lie in Japan, where the shortage of courses means that many golfers may never actually play on one, only on driving ranges. But they do this in growing numbers and with fanatical devotion. The ranges are often not attractive places so one must conclude that in part it is the sheer pleasure of hitting the ball and seeing it soar off that makes golf so compulsive. Swing the club and send the ball flying to its target. This is the basic delight of the game, played on all kinds of courses by all kinds of people, a test of oneself and certainly the pleasantest way of meeting new friends.

Golf, surely, for whatever reason, often becomes an obsession, and a very genial one. Long may it be so!

(right) Alexander McKellar, the fanatical 'Cock o' the Green', a late-comer to golf who became so addicted that he played in the dark by lantern light.

(next page, right) St Andrews, the cradle of golf and home of the Royal and Ancient Golf Club. This view shows the Home Hole, with clubhouse and town buildings in the background, one of the best-known scenes to golfers.

COCK OF THE GREEN.

Winners

British Open Championship

1860 Willie Park Sen.	1890 John Ball Jun.	1924 Walter Hagen	1959 Gary J. Player
1861 Tom Morris Sen.	1891 Hugh Kirkaldy	1925 Jim Barnes	1960 Kel D. G. Nagle
1862 Tom Morris Sen.	1892 Harold H. Hilton	1926 Robert T. Jones Jun.	1961 Arnold Palmer
1863 Willie Park Sen.	1893 Willie Auchterlonie	1927 Robert T. Jones Jun.	1962 Arnold Palmer
1864 Tom Morris Sen.	1894 John Henry Taylor	1928 Walter Hagen	1963 Bob J. Charles
1865 Andrew Strath	1895 John Henry Taylor	1929 Walter Hagen	1964 Tony Lema
1866 Willie Park Sen.	1896 Harry Vardon	1930 Robert T. Jones Jun.	1965 Peter W. Thompson
1867 Tom Morris Sen.	1897 Harold H. Hilton	1931 Tommy D. Armour	1966 Jack Nicklaus
1868 Tom Morris Jun.	1898 Harry Vardon	1932 Gene Sarazen	1967 Roberto di Vicenzo
1869 Tom Morris Jun.	1899 Harry Vardon	1933 Densmore Shute	1968 Gary J. Player
1870 Tom Morris Jun.	1900 John Henry Taylor	1934 T. Henry Cotton	1969 Tony Jacklin
1872 Tom Morris Jun.	1901 James Braid	1935 Alfred Perry	1970 Jack Nicklaus
1873 Tom Kidd	1902 Alex Herd	1936 Alf H. Padgham	1971 Lee Trevino
1874 Mungo Park	1903 Harry Vardon	1937 T. Henry Cotton	1972 Lee Trevino
1875 Willie Park Sen.	1904 Jack White	1938 Reg A. Whitcombe	1973 Tom Weiskopf
1876 Bob Martin	1905 James Braid	1939 Richard Burton	1974 Gary J. Player
1877 Jamie Anderson	1906 James Braid	1946 Sam Snead	1975 Tom Watson
1878 Jamie Anderson	1907 Arnaud Massey	1947 Fred Daly	1976 Johnnie Miller
1879 Jamie Anderson	1908 James Braid	1948 T. Henry Cotton	1977 Tom Watson
1880 Bob Ferguson	1909 John Henry Taylor	1949 Bobby Locke	1978 Jack Nicklaus
1881 Bob Ferguson	1910 James Braid	1950 Bobby Locke	1979 Severiano Ballesteros
1882 Bob Ferguson	1911 Harry Vardon	1951 Max Faulkner	1980 Tom Watson
1883 Willie Fernie	1912 Edward Ray	1952 Bobby Locke	1981 Bud Rogers
1884 Jack Simpson	1913 John Henry Taylor	1953 Ben Hogan	1982 Tom Watson
1885 Bob Martin	1914 Harry Vardon	1954 Peter W. Thompson	1983 Tom Watson
1886 David Brown	1920 George Duncan	1955 Peter W. Thompson	1984 Severiano Ballesteros
1887 Willie Park Jun.	1921 Jock Hutchinson	1956 Peter W. Thompson	1985 Sandy Lyle
1888 Jack Burns	1922 Walter Hagen	1957 Bobby Locke	1986 Greg Norman
1889 Willie Park Jun.	1923 Arthur G. Havers	1958 Peter W. Thompson	

US Open Championship

1895 Horace Rawlins	1916 Charles Evans Jun.	1940 Lawson Little	1966 Billy Casper
1896 James Foulis	1919 Walter Hagen	1941 Craig Wood	1967 Jack Nicklaus
1897 Joe Lloyd	1920 Edward Ray	1946 Lloyd Mangrum	1968 Lee Trevino
1898 Fred Herd	1921 Jim Barnes	1947 Lew Worsham	1969 Orville J. Moody
1899 Willie Smith	1922 Gene Sarazen	1948 Ben Hogan	1970 Tony Jacklin
1900 Harry Vardon	1923 Robert T. Jones	1949 Cary Middlecoff	1971 Lee Trevino
1901 Willie Anderson	1924 Cyril Walker	1950 Ben Hogan	1972 Jack Nicklaus
1902 Lawrence Auchterlonie	1925 Willie MacFarlane	1951 Ben Hogan	1973 Johnny Miller
1903 Willie Anderson	1926 Robert T. Jones	1952 Julius Boros	1974 Hale Irwin
1904 Willie Anderson	1927 Tommy Armour	1953 Ben Hogan	1975 Lou Graham
1905 Willie Anderson	1928 Johnny Farrell	1954 Ed Furgol	1976 Jack Pate
1906 Alex Smith	1929 Robert T. Jones	1955 Jack Fleck	1977 Hubert M. Green
1907 Alex Ross	1930 Robert T. Jones	1956 Cary Middlecoff	1978 Andy North
1908 Fred McLeod	1931 Billy Burke	1957 Dick Mayer	1979 Hale Irwin
1909 George Sargent	1932 Gene Sarazen	1958 Tommy Bolt	1980 Jack Nicklaus
1910 Alex Smith	1933 Johnny Goodman	1959 Billy Casper	1981 David Graham
1911 John McDermott	1934 Olin Dutra	1960 Arnold Palmer	1982 Tom Watson
1912 John McDermott	1935 Sam Parks	1961 Gene Littler	1983 Larry Nelson
1913 Francis Ouimet	1936 Tony Mamero	1962 Jack Nicklaus	1984 Fuzzy Zoeller
1914 Walter Hagen	1937 Ralph Guldahl	1963 Julius Boros	1985 Andy North
1915 Jerome D. Travers	1938 Ralph Guldahl	1964 Ken Venturi	1986 Raymond Floyd
	1939 Byron Nelson	1965 Gary Player	

Bibliography

The following is a selection of some of the numerous books and publications on the history of golf. In writing this book the author has also made frequent reference to early and recent editions of newspapers, magazines and annuals, including in particular *Golf Illustrated*, *Golf Monthly* and *The Golfer's Handbook*, all published in London, and *Golf Magazine*, published in New York.

Adamson, Alistair, *In the Wind's Eye: The North Berwick Golf Club* (Edinburgh 1980)

Braid, James, *Advanced Golf* (London, 1908)

Clark, Robert, *Golf, a Royal and Ancient Game* (London, 1893)

Darwin, Bernard, *Golf* (London, 1954)

Darwin, Bernard, *Golf between the Wars* (London, 1944)

Darwin, Bernard, *The Golf Courses of the British Isles* (London, 1910)

Darwin, B., Longhurst, H., Cotton, H., *et al.*, *A History of Golf in Britain* (London, 1952)

Davis, William (ed.), *The Punch Book of Golf* (London, 1973)

Hagen, Walter, *The Walter Hagen Story* (London, 1957)

Henderson, I. T. and Stirk, D. I., *Golf in the Making* (Winchester, Hants, 1979)

Henderson, I. T. and Stirk, D. I., *Royal Blackheath* (London, 1981)

van Hengel, Steven J. H., *Early Golf* (Liechtenstein, 1985)

Hezlet, May, *Ladies' Golf* (London, 1907)

Hilton, Harold, and Smith, Garden G., *The Royal and Ancient Game of Golf* (Edinburgh, 1912)

Hutchinson, Horace G., *The Badminton Library: Golf* (London, 1892)

Mortimer, Charles G. and Pignon, Fred, *The Story of the Open Golf Championship* (London, 1952)

Nicklaus, Jack, *The Greatest Game of All* (New York, 1969)

Ouimet, Francis, *A Game of Golf* (London and New York, n.d.)

Park, W. Jun., *The Game of Golf* (London, 1896)

Plimpton, George, *The Bogey Man* (London, 1969)

Pottinger, George, *Muirfield and the Honourable Company* (Edinburgh, 1972)

Ryde, Peter, *The Royal and Ancient Championship Records, 1860-1980* (St Andrews, 1981)

Simpson, Sir Walter, *The Art of Golf* (Edinburgh, 1892)

Steel, Donald, *The Guinness Book of Golf Facts and Figures* (London, 1980)

Tulloch, W. W., *The Life of Tom Morris* (reprinted London, 1982)

Vardon, Harry, *The Complete Golfer* (London, 1905)

Ward-Thomas, P., *The Royal and Ancient* (St Andrews, 1980)

Wild, Roland, *The Loneliest Game* (Vancouver, 1969)

Wood, Harry B., *Golfing Curios and 'the Like'* (first published 1911; reprinted Manchester 1980)

Index

Acknowledgements

The author gratefully acknowledges the assistance of
Edward Davies in preparing the essay on *The Clubmaker's
Craft* and the assistance of Donald Steel in preparing the
essay on *Creating a Golf Course.*

The publishers wish to thank all private owners, photographers, museums, galleries, libraries, Golf Clubs and
other institutions for their help in obtaining photographs
and the permission to reproduce them. Particular thanks
are extended to Sarah Baddicl; the Royal and Ancient Golf
Club, St Andrews; and the Royal North Devon Golf Club,
Westward Ho! Further acknowledgement is made to the
following (t = top, b = bottom, l = left, r = right):

© ADAGP: 143; ALLSPORT/Dave Cannon: 126; Amsterdam City Record Office (Topographical Atlas): 17(3); Sarah
Baddiel Collection, Gray's Antique Market, London: 59;
Sarah Baddiel collection/photos David Cripps: jacket front,
1, 2, 17(4), 21(t), 24, 34, 64, 65, 67, 68(t,b), 70, 75, 79, 83,
84(t), 86, 87, 88(1), © the estate of the late H. M. Bateman
88(2), 88(4), 89(5), 103, 153; Archie Baird Collection, East
Lothian: 3, 7, 26, 27, 123; BBC Hulton Picture Library: 105,
109(3), 117, 120, 132(4,5), 81(3,6,9); Chris Beetles Ltd.,
London: 85, © Heath Robinson Estate 102; British Library,
London: 10(t); Centraal Museum, Utrecht: 17(5); City
Musea of Gouda: 16(2); Christie's, London: 18,19; Peter
Dazeley, London: 45, 50(4), 80(1), 81(5), 124, 128, 132(2),
133(6), 136(t,b), 137(t), 138(b), 141(t), 148, 149, 155; Sonia
Halliday Photographs/by courtesy of the Dean and Chapter
of Gloucester Cathedral: 10(b); Henderson & Stirk Ltd.:
12(t); Honourable Company of Edinburgh Golfers,
Muirfield: 62, 69, 73; Illustrated London News Photo
Library: 60, 114(1); Lawrence Levy/Yours in Sport: 132(1),
138(t), 140; Lisa Leighton, Score Magazine, Toronto:
135; Lord's Gallery, London: 107; Mansell Collection,
London: 80(2); Minneapolis Institute of Arts/William Hood
Dunwoody Fund: 6–7; Mizuno Golf Clubs/AMPM: 46–7;
Brian Morgan, Glasgow: 121(t); Museum Boymans van
Beuningen, Rotterdam: 39; National Gallery, London:
11; Pau Golf Club, France: 58; Phaidon Press: 77, 108(1);
Phaidon Press/photos David Cripps: 36–7(1–6); Photo
Source, London: 81(7); Private Collection, London/© Mrs
Barbara Edwards and the estate of the late Arthur Rackham:
5, 91; Private Collection, Paris: 118, 119; © Punch Mag-
azines 88(3); By kind permission of the Queen's Body
Guard for Scotland (Royal Company of Archers): 63;
Rijksmuseum, Amsterdam: 21; By kind permission of the
Royal and Ancient Golf Club of St Andrews, Fife: 16(1), 30,
51(5), 81(10), © the estate of the late H. M. Bateman 89(6),
92, 108(2), 116(t), 120(t); By kind permission of the Royal
and Ancient Golf Club of St Andrews, Fife/photos David
Cripps: 13, 14, 29, 31, 33(t), 40(l,r), 43, 44, 49(t,b), 53, 54, 55,
66, 71, 82, 98, 99, 101, 106(t,b), 109(4,5); Scottish National
Portrait Gallery, Edinburgh: 22, 23; © Phil Sheldon: jacket
back, 94, 110–11, 122, 129, 130–1, 133(3), 137(b), 139, 141(r),
142(Jan Traylen), 146–7, 150–1; Sotheby's, London: 12(b),
15, 61, 84; Donald Steel: 144–5; David Stirk Collection: 8,
33(b), 50(1), 57, 81(4,8), 90, 97, 100, 113, 114(2,3), David
Stirk Collection/photos David Cripps: 35, 42, 54, 74, 78,
115(4); St Andrew's University Library, Cowie Collection:
28, 32, 50(2,3), 52 (t,b), 72, 76, 109(6), 112, 116(b), 121(b),
133(7); Patrick Ward, London: 127, 134.